T5-COD-773

Yuko Takagi
Contemporary Floral Art

stichting kunstboek

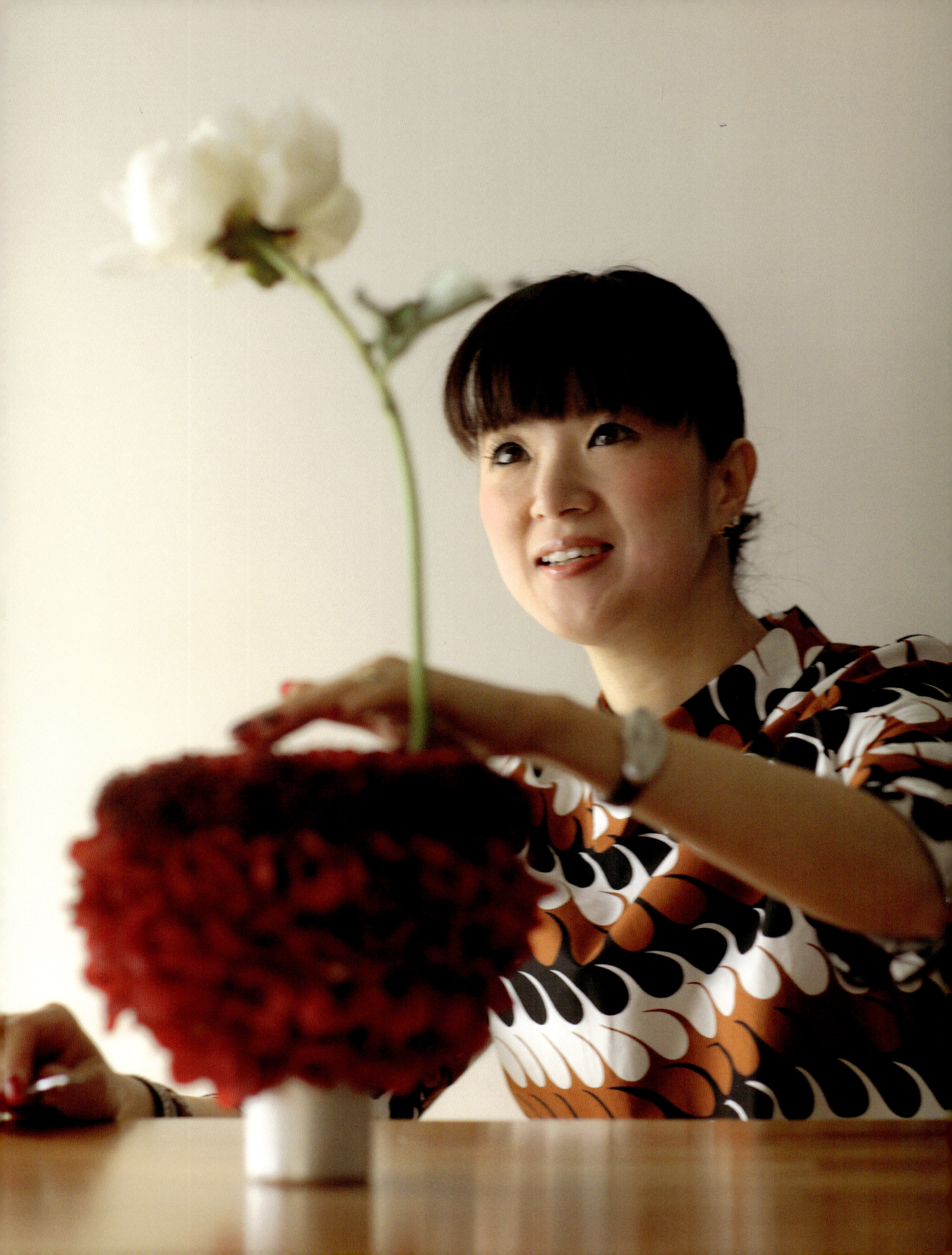

25 years have gone by since my decision to live with flowers,
a time filled with cheerfulness and warmth
sometimes difficult and with a bitter heart,
a period as diverse as the four seasons
and colorful as life itself.

Various encounters and experiences
brought me to today,
loved by people
loving people
backed up by people
and nurtured by people.

My passion for plants
is equal to my love for people,
it's grand and deep,
and without limits.

I would like to thank countless
friends, family and colleagues
who taught me everything I know in life,
I am grateful for being born in Japan
with its wonderful culture and beautiful scenery.

I feel gratitude and contentment
and would like to continue giving
to plants and people,
carry on an affectionate
and gentle way of living.

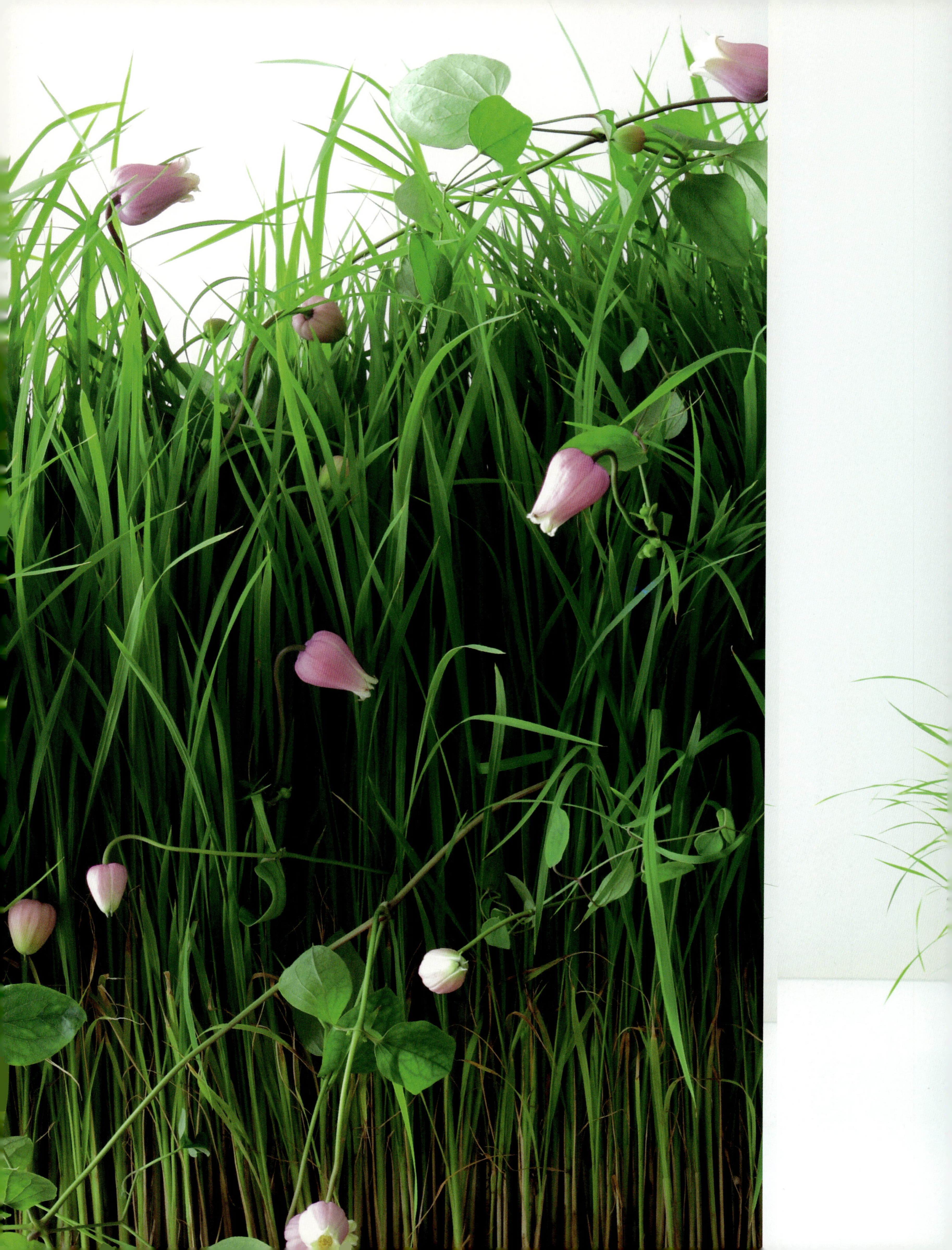

The rice plant
companion of Man since ancient times,
its beauty as pure and true
as Japan's scenery,
as the culture it's been nurturing.

Clematis integrifolia / Oryza sativa

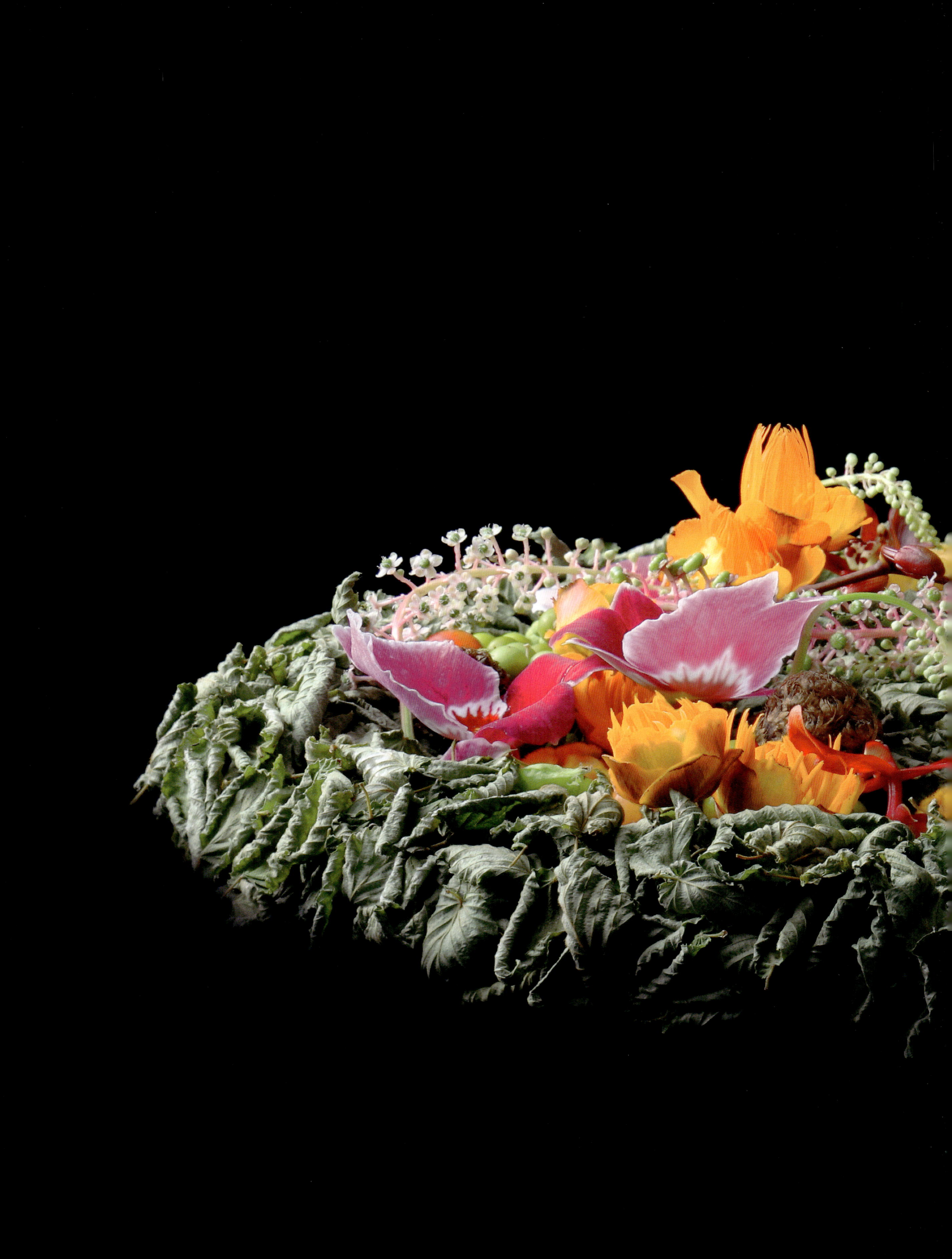

Anthurium / Celosia cristata / Miltonia / Mokara / Phytolacca americana / Physalis pubescens / Prunus avium / Smilax glabra / Swida controversa / Trollius

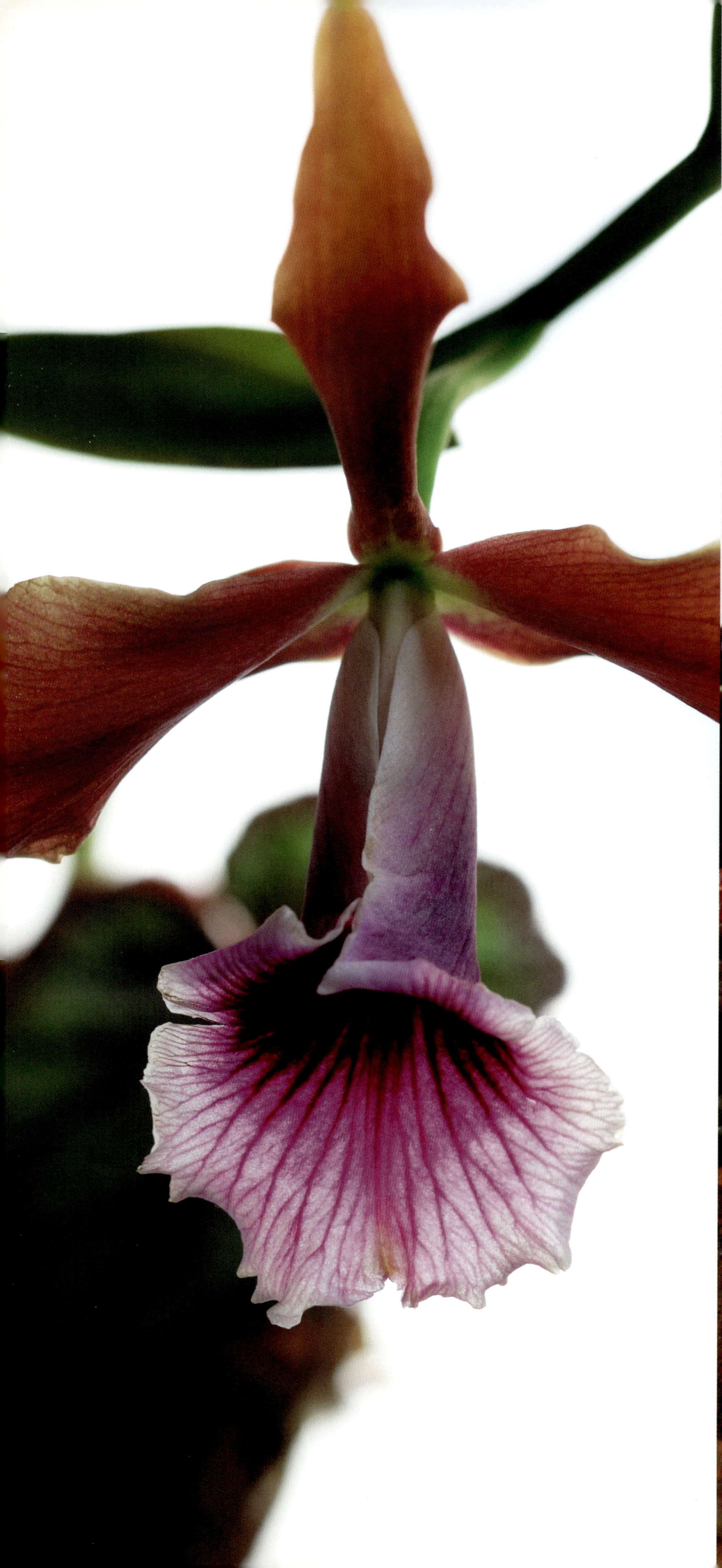
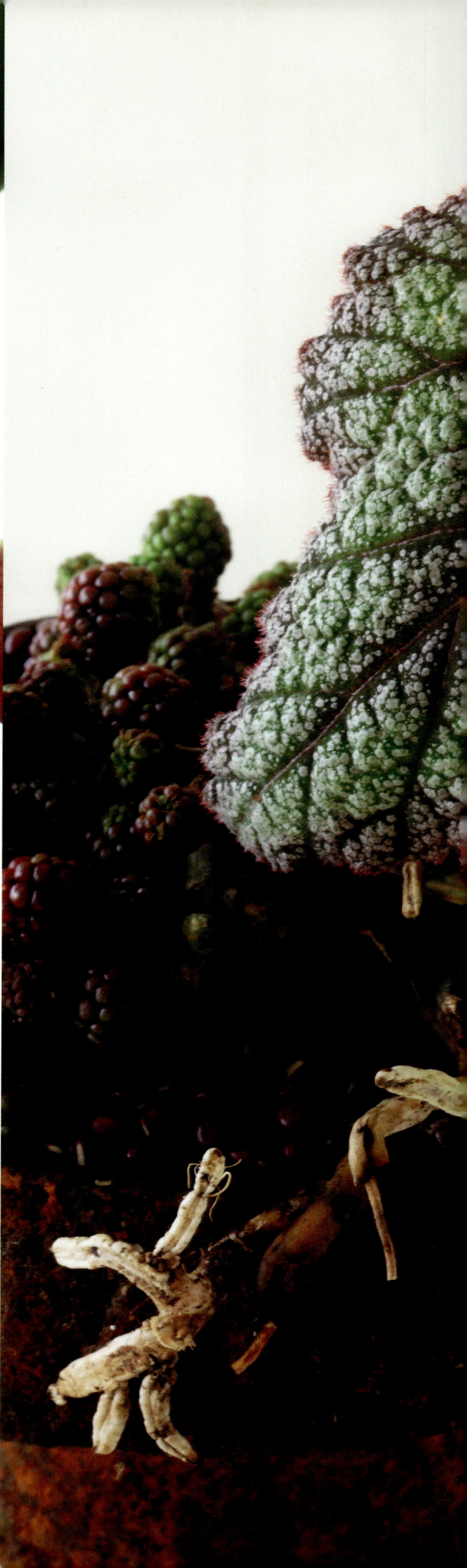

Laelia tenebrosa 'Rain Forest' / Pelargonium x hortorum /
Rubus fruticosus / Nepenthes / Vigna angularis

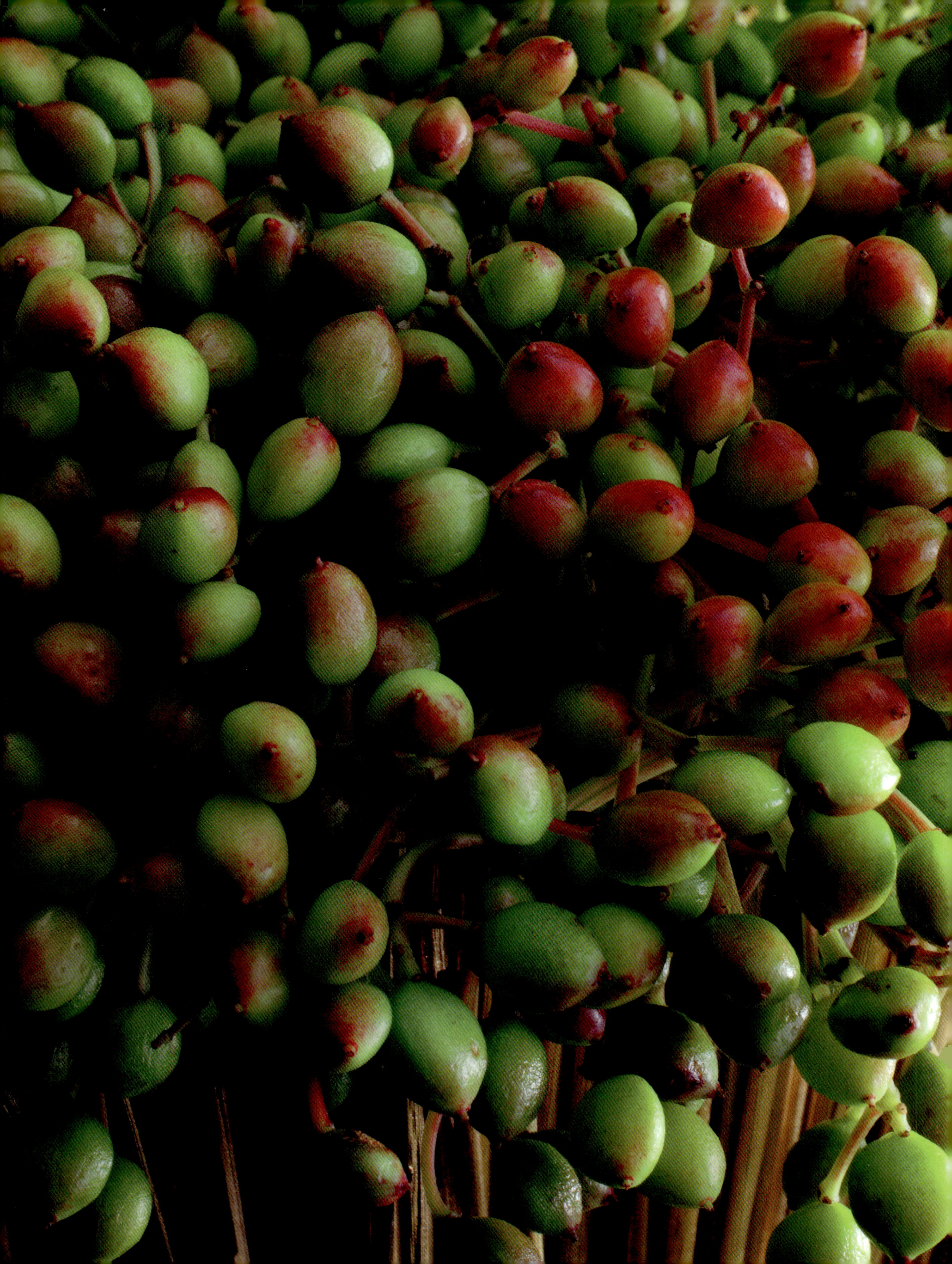

12 | 13

Brassia Eternal Wind 'Summer Dream' /
Pelargonium x hortorum /
Viburnum compactum

Eucharis grandiflora / Peperomia

Made with no other intention
than being thrown away
the material is reborn
and brought to life
by adding one single flower.

Begonia / Chrysanthemum cinerariifolium / Eucalyptus tetragona / Lagenaria siceraria var. nispida /
Myrtaceae / Odontoglossum / Prunus mume / Tillandsia xerographica

16 | 17

The beauty and grace
of one single orchid is
even sweeter and more refined
than sugar crystals.

Phalaenopsis / Tillandsia xerographica Rohweder

Clematis integrifolia / Hoya carnosa / Phalaenopsis / Phytolacca americana

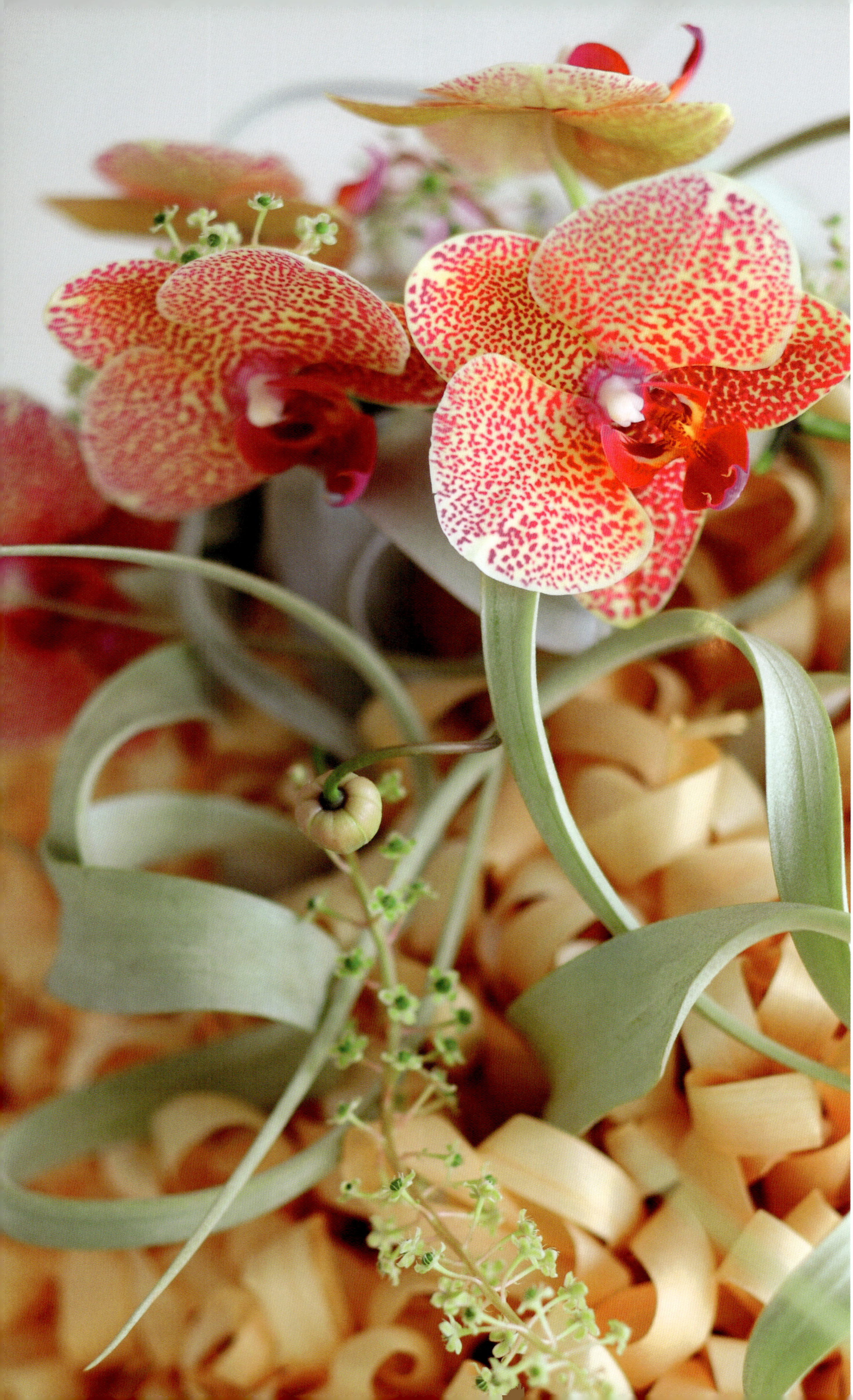

Clematis integrifolia / Hoya carnosa / Phalaenopsis /
Phytolacca americana / Tillandsia xerographica Rohweder

Paederia scandens

22 | 23

Clematis hybrid

A thousand years of life
crystallized salt into a rock
one orchid root
reaches out
and embraces history.

Orchidaceae

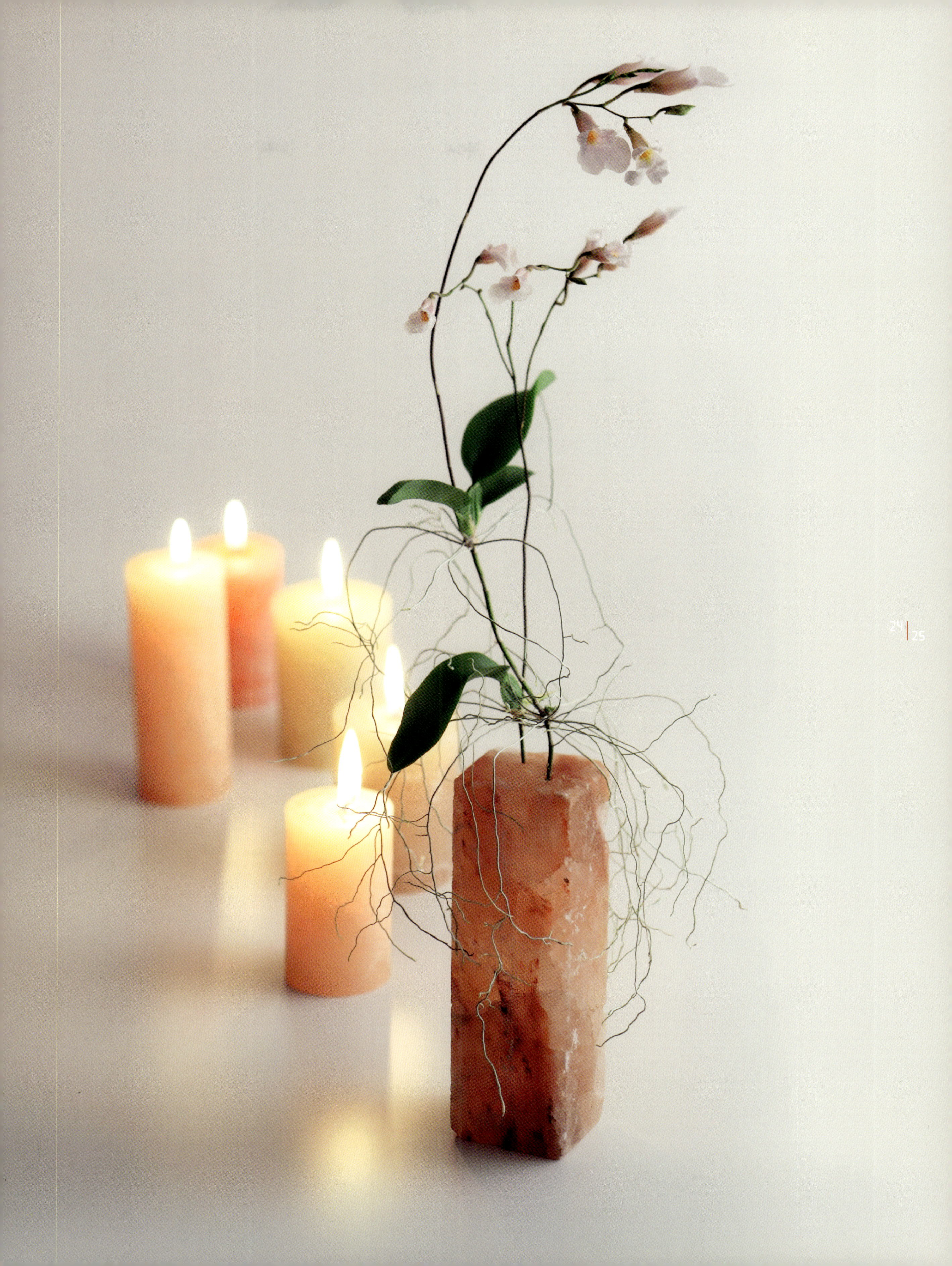

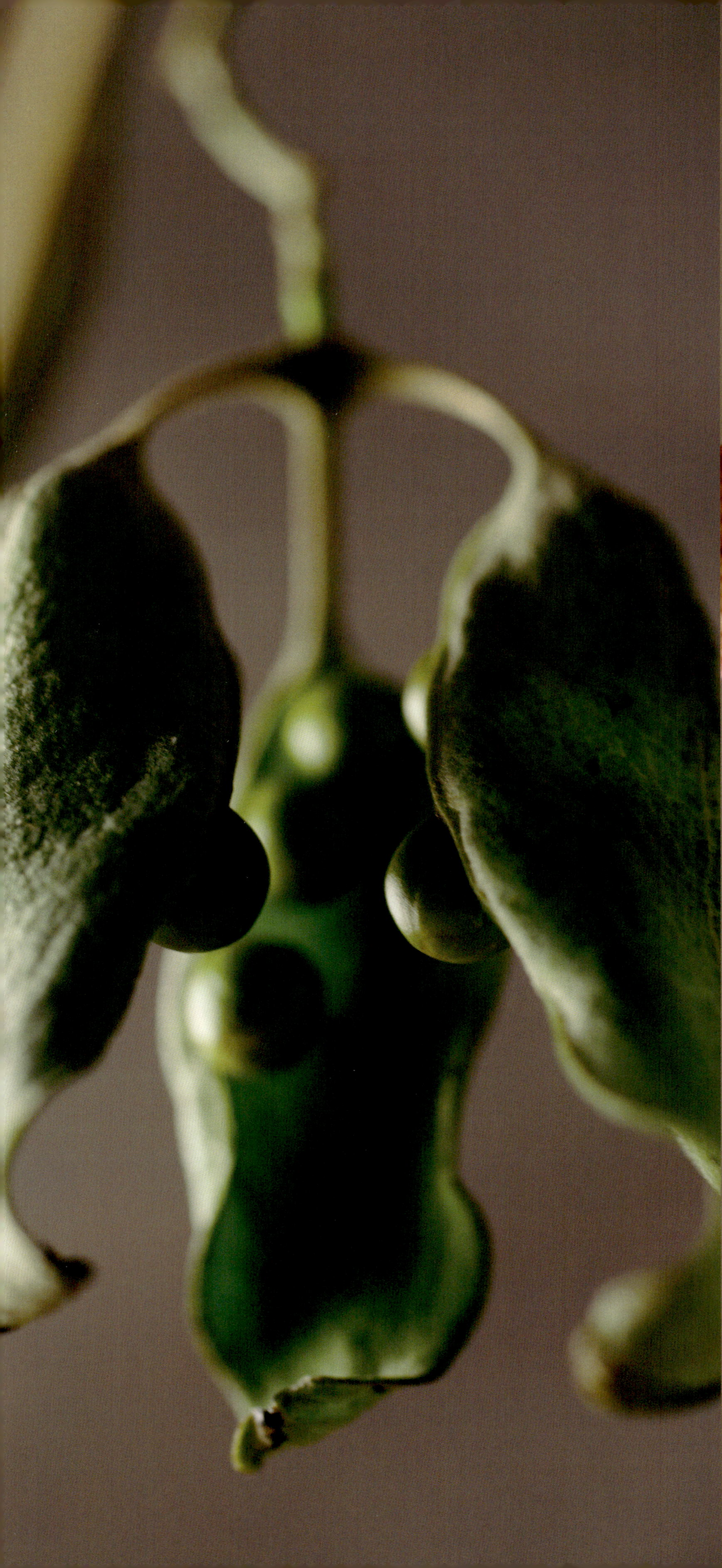
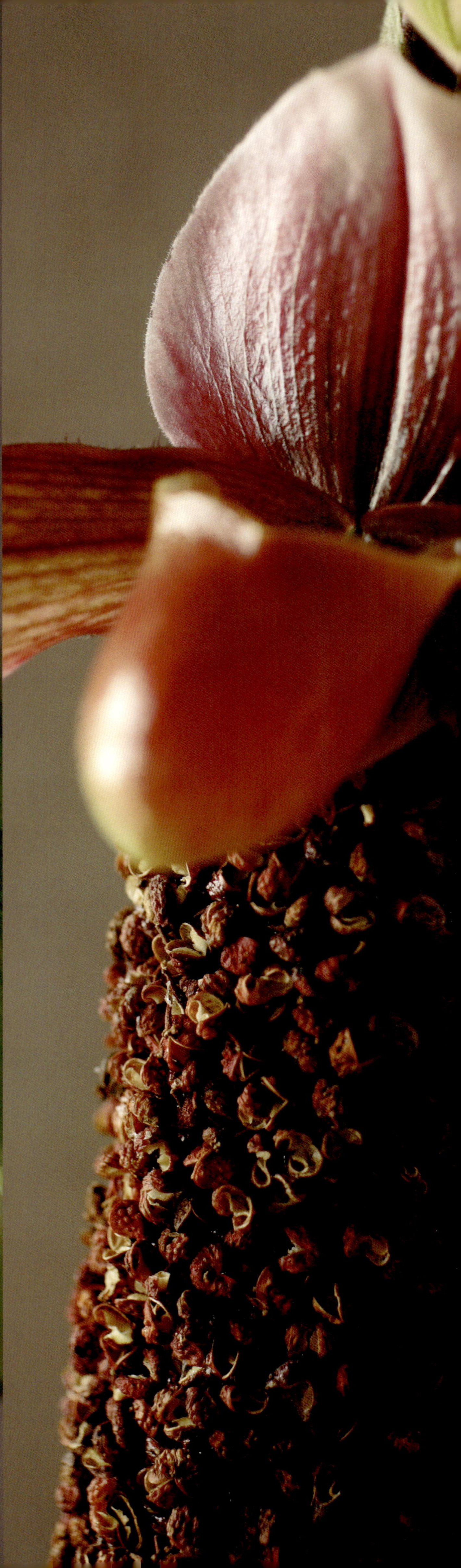

Maxillaria tenuifolium / Phalaenopsis /
Rivina humilis / Vigna radiata

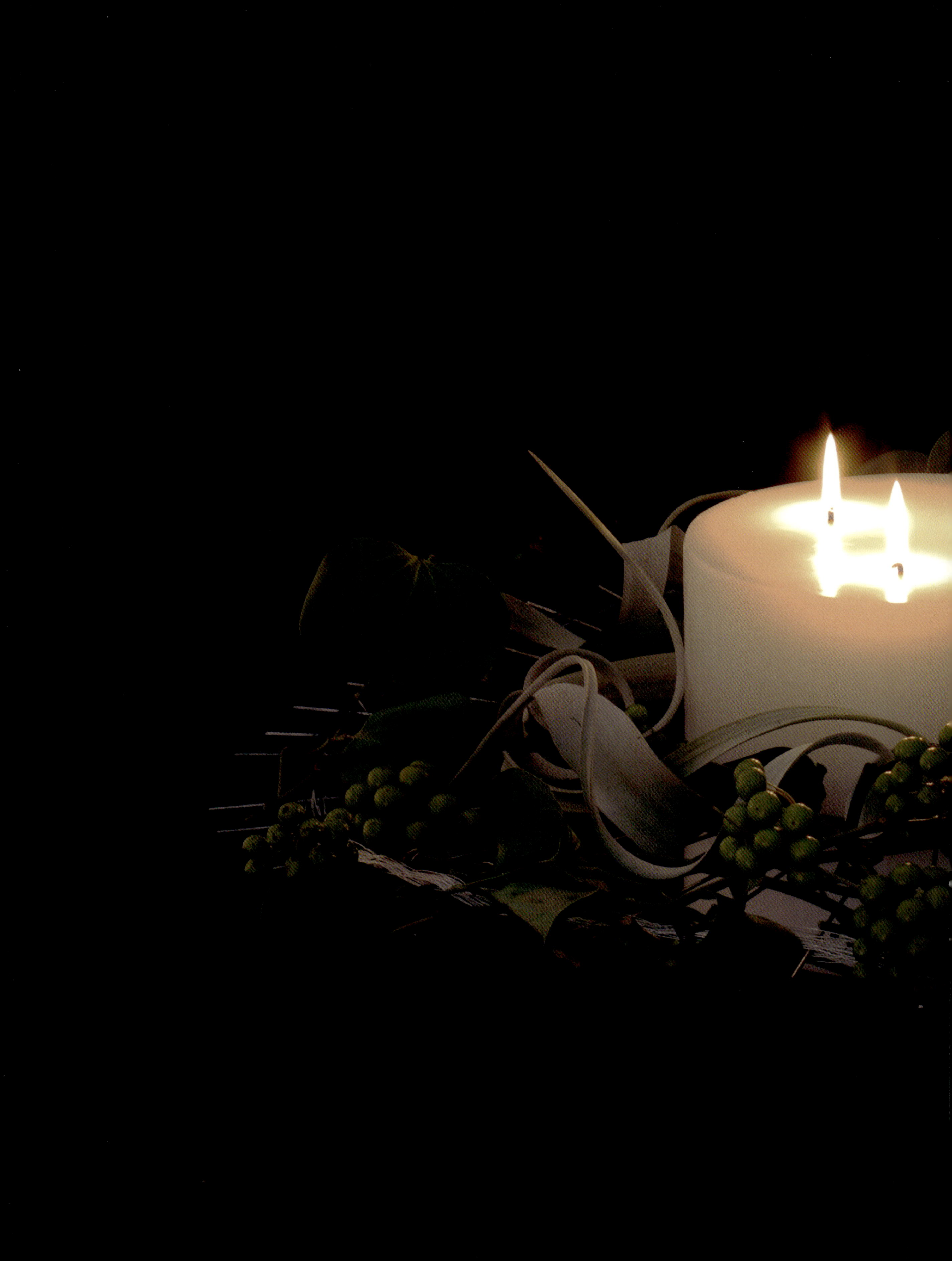

Smilax glabra / Tillandsia xerographica Rohweder

Bright colors and astonishing shapes.
Even without artful adjustments
and designer's interventions
plants have surprisingly strong features
and individual characters.

Maxillaria tenuifolium / *Phalaenopsis* /
Rivina humilis / *Vigna radiata*

Capsicum annuum / Ceropegia woodii / Echevaria / Eucalyptus tetragona / Hydrangea /
Rubus / Smilax aspera / Vanda 'Mokara' / Vigna radiata

32 | 33

Anigozanthos / Orchidaceae

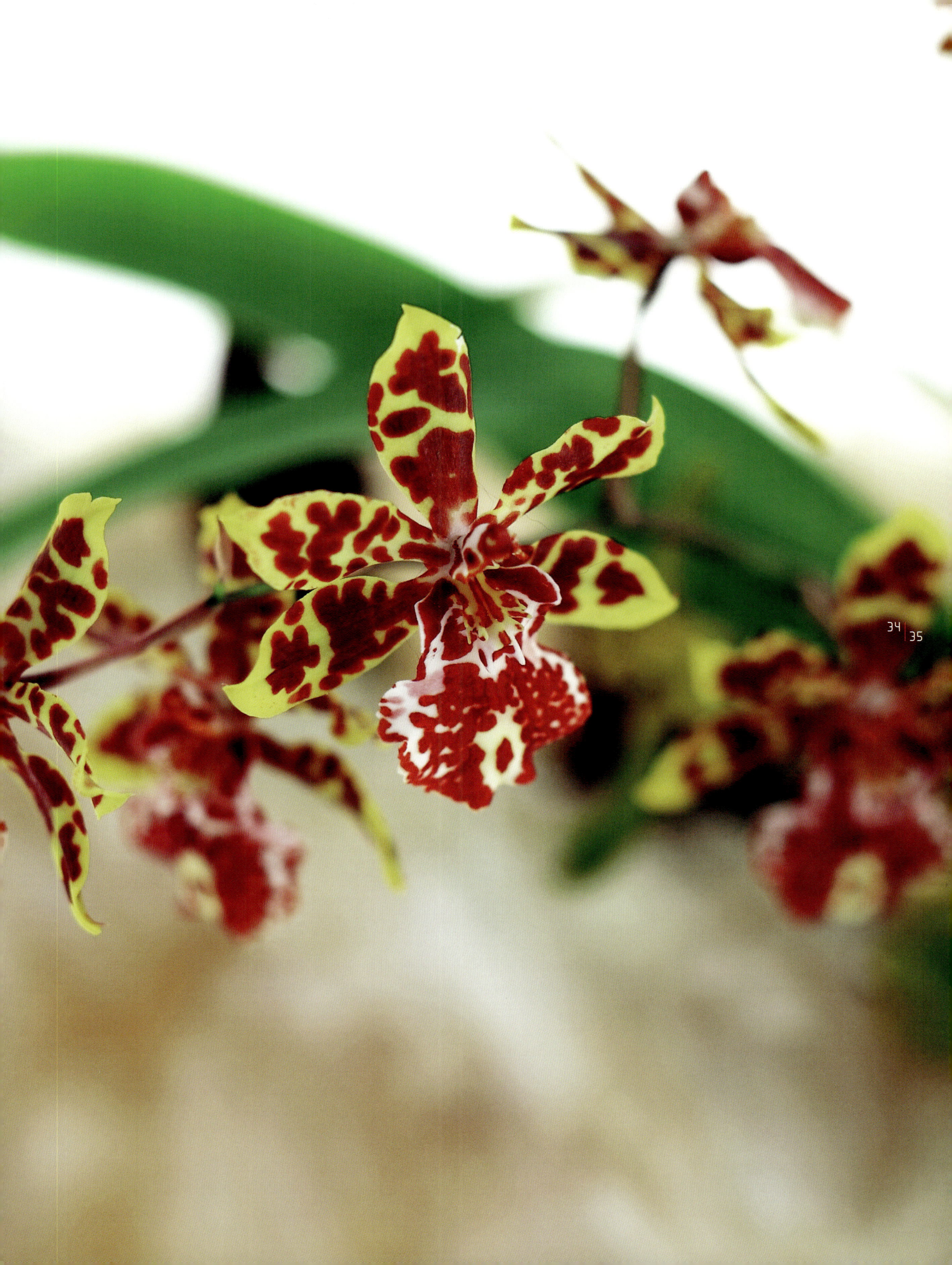

Pieces of shattered glass and a glass container.
Even though it is the same material,
one is worthless and one is valued.
They are equal to the flower,
outshining both of them.

Hedera / Phalaenopsis

Cymbidium / Hedera / Rosa multiflora

Playful orchids
rustle and whiffle
like paper ribbons.

Anigozanthos / Orchidaceae

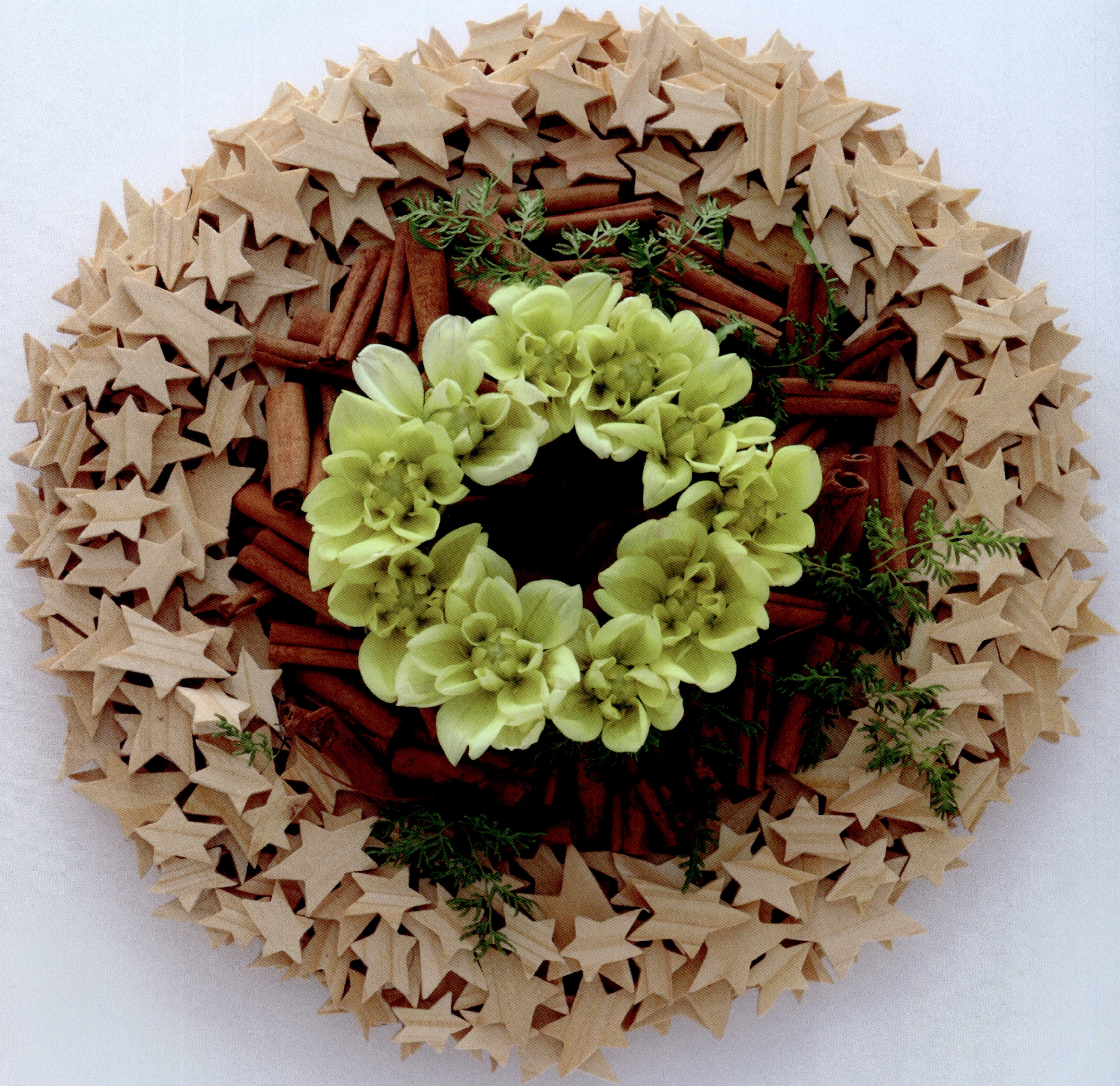

Dahlia x cultorum / Pteridophyta

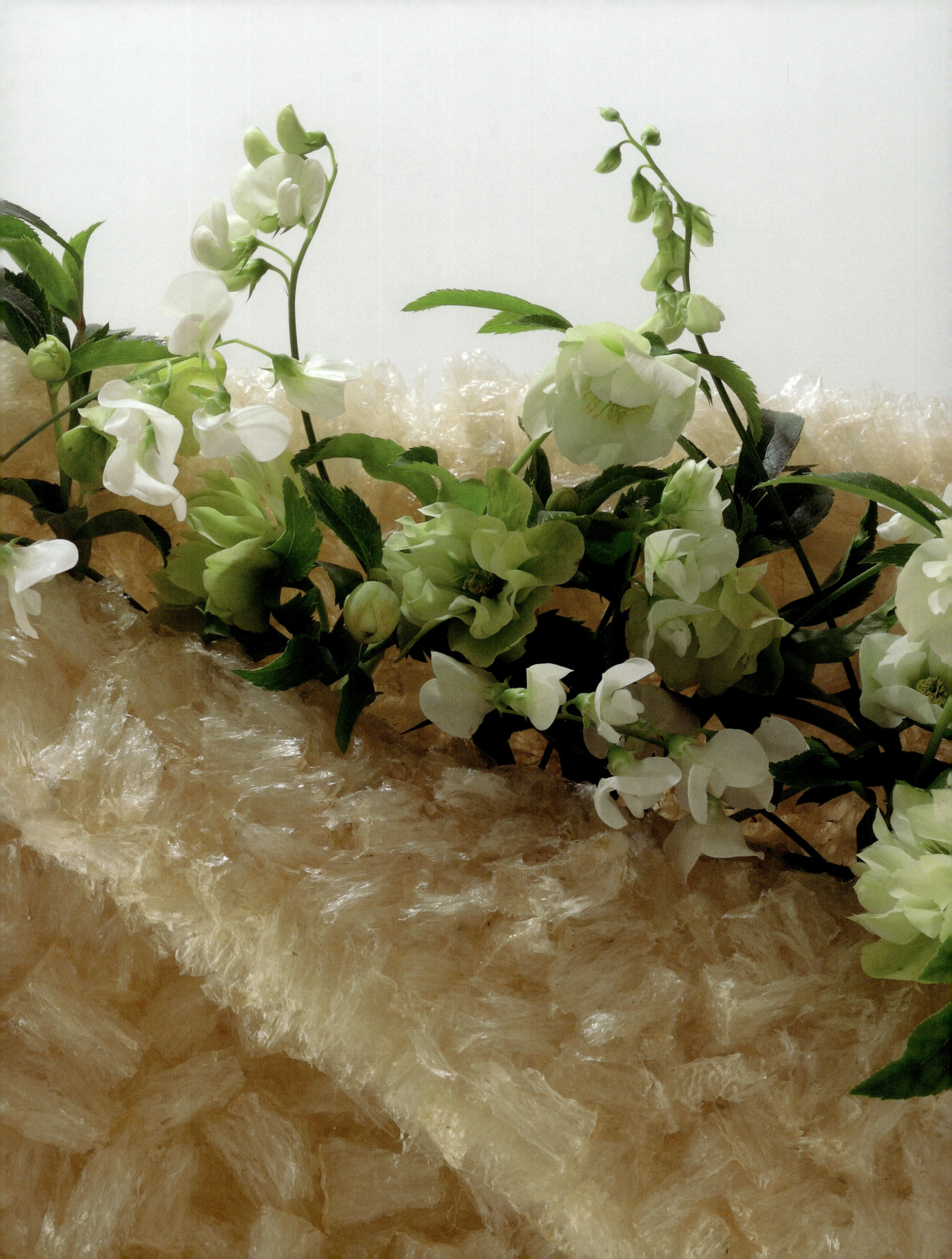

Helleborus orientalis / Lathyrus odoratus

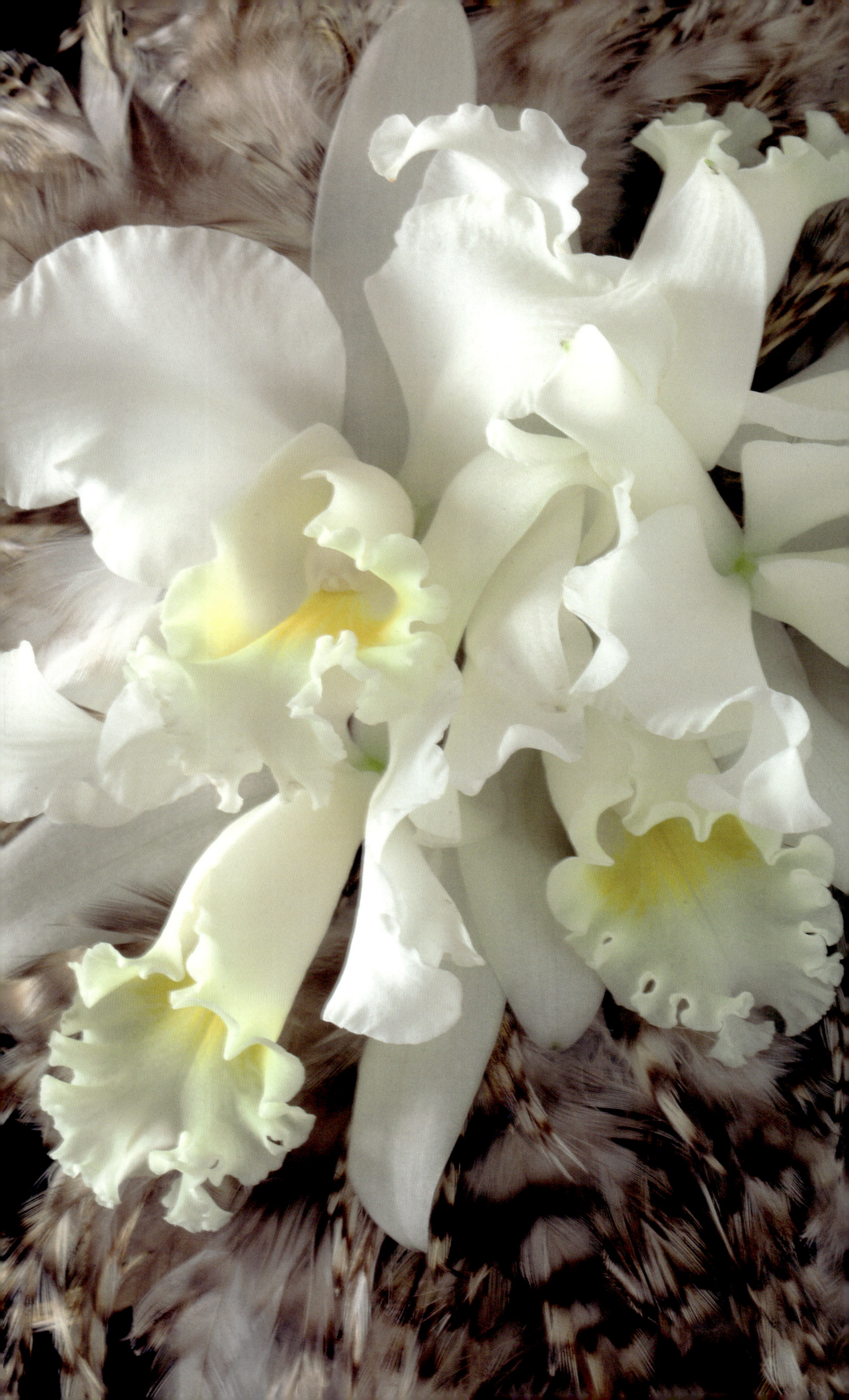

Cattleya labiata

Walk through town
as a stylish icon
the head held high
like a spring flower
smiling at the sun.

Begonia / Eucalyptus / Phytolacca americana /
Tillandsia xerographica Rohweder / Zygopetalum Redvale 'Pretty Ann'

46 | 47

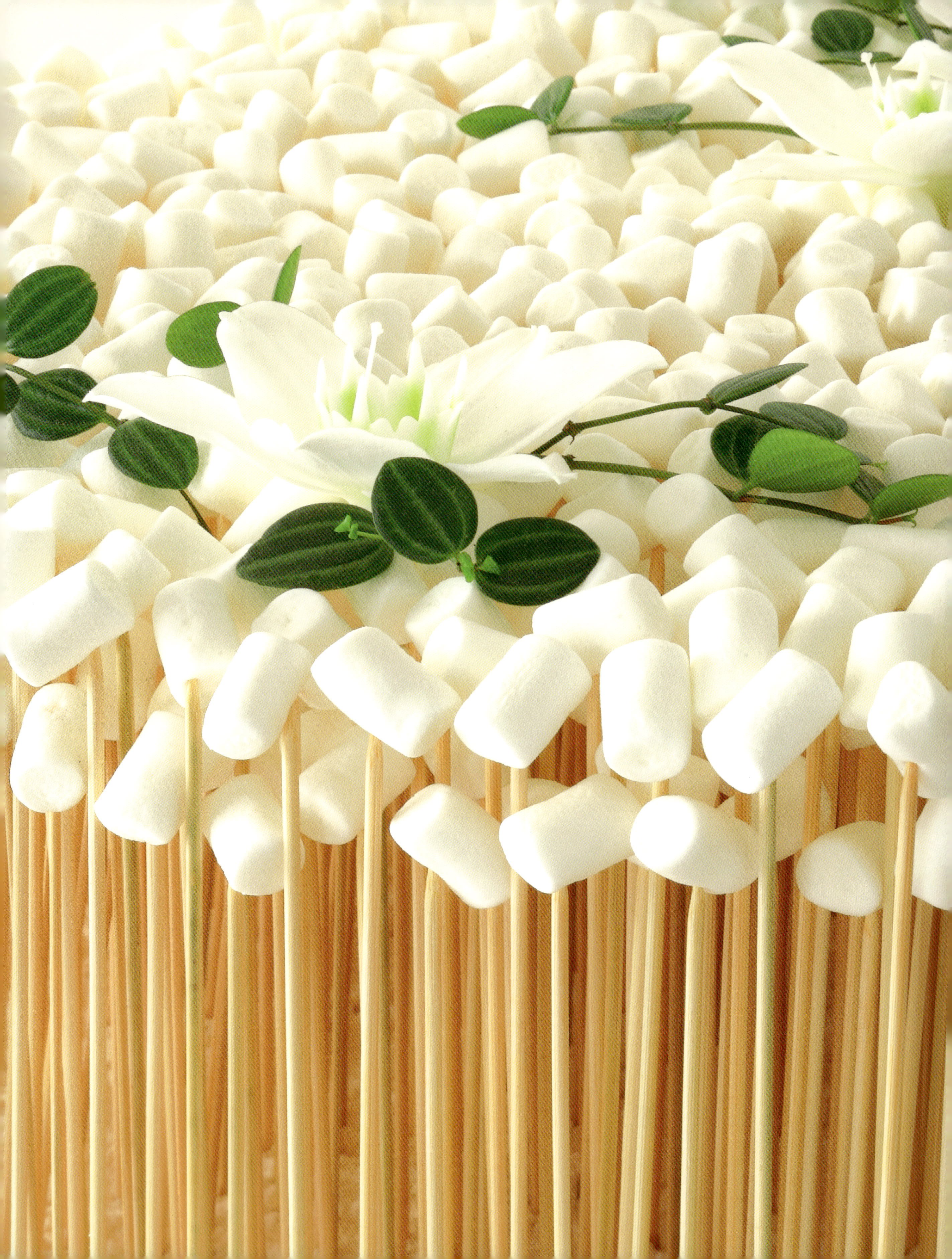

Eucharis grandiflora / Peperomia

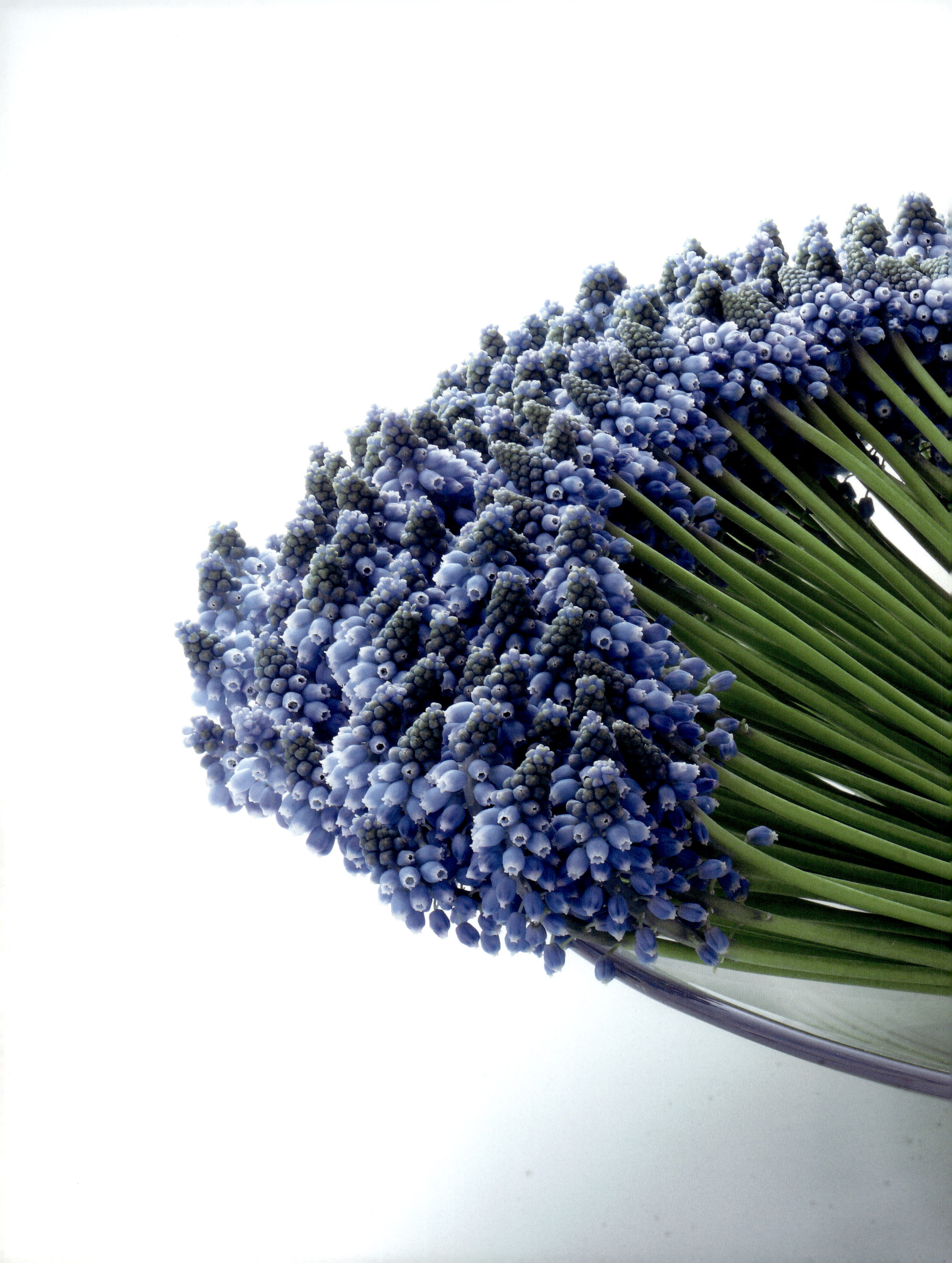

Muscari armeniacum

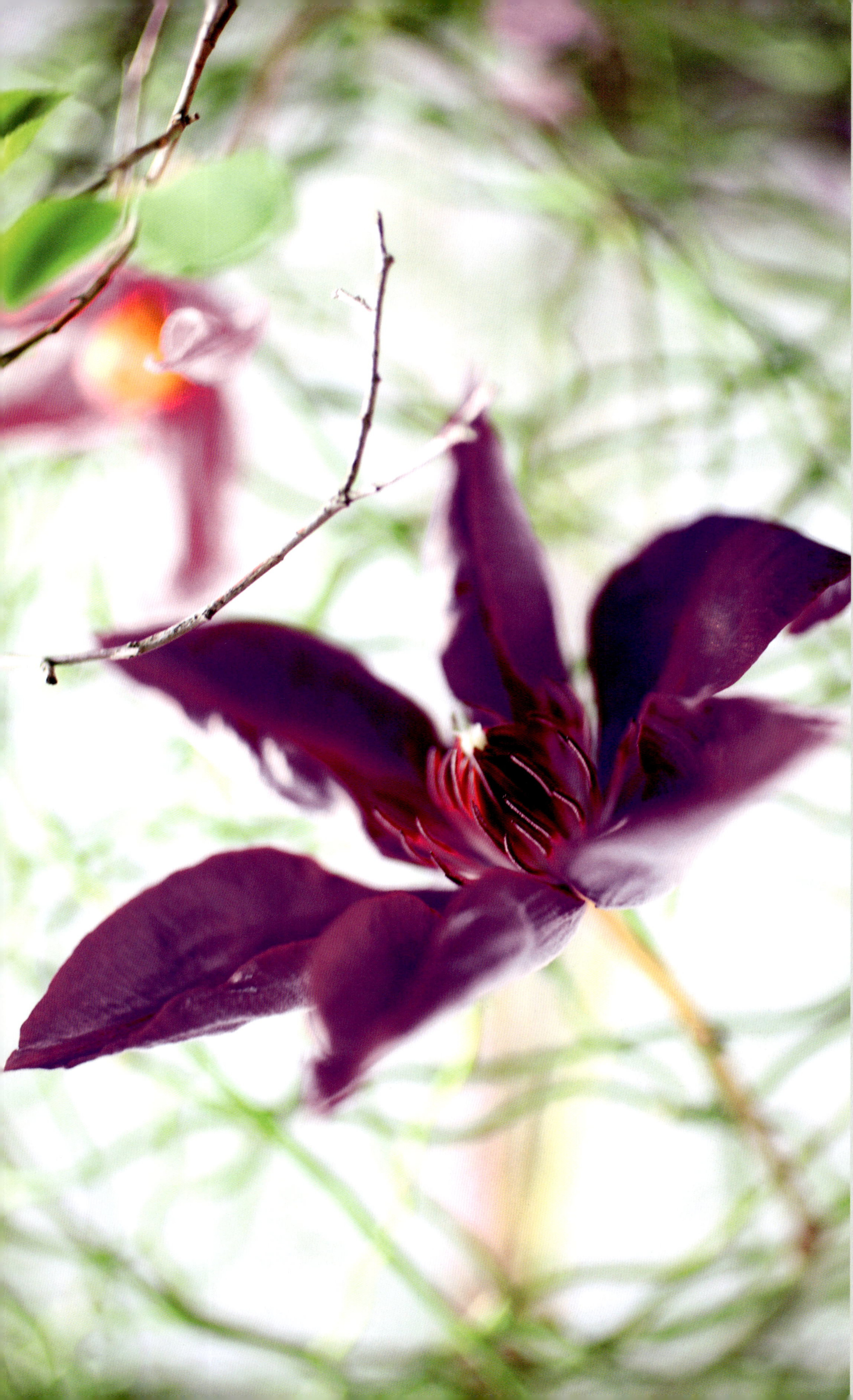

52 | 53

Asparagus asparagoides / Clematis florida /
Clematis integrifolia / Vaccinium oldhamii

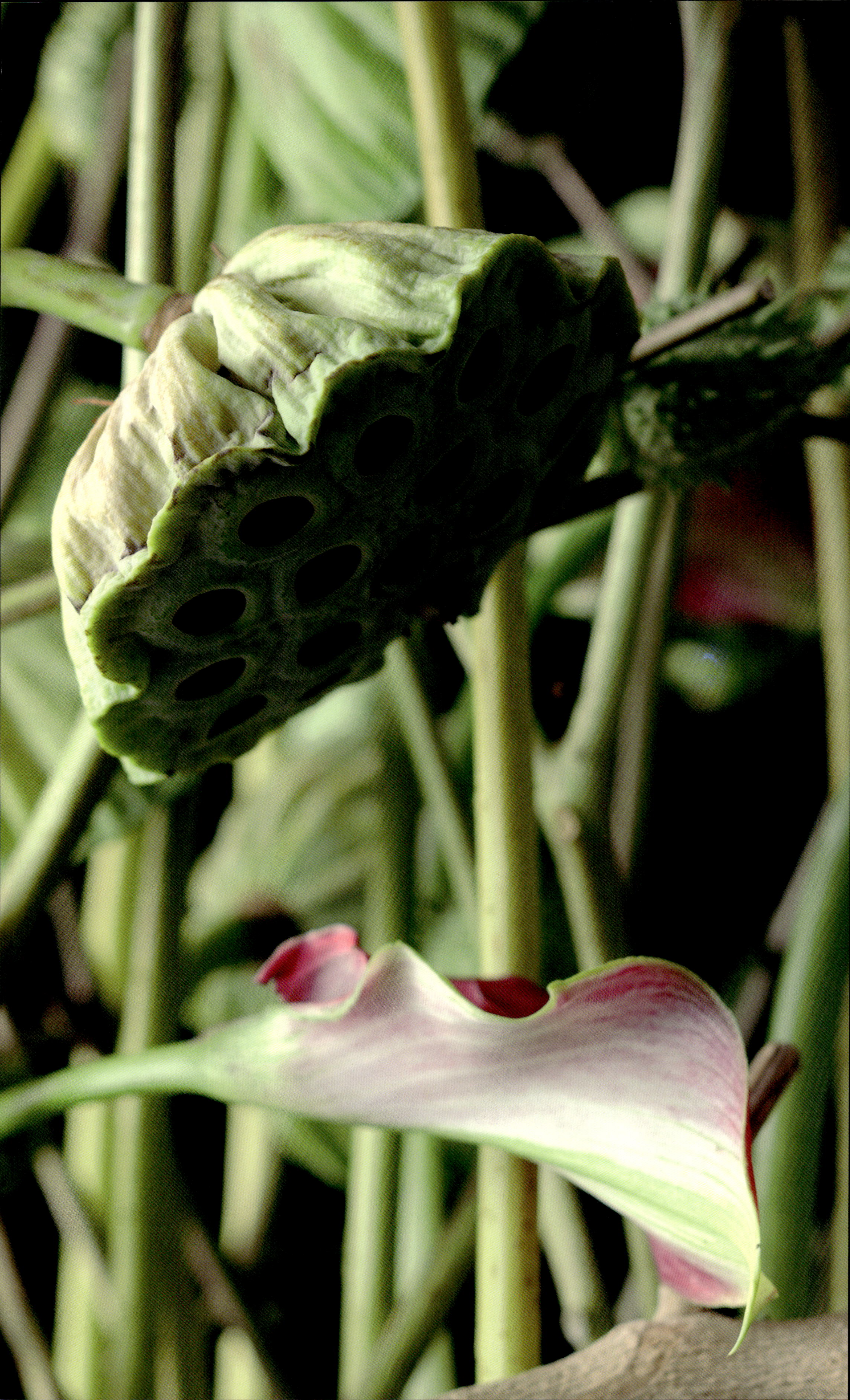
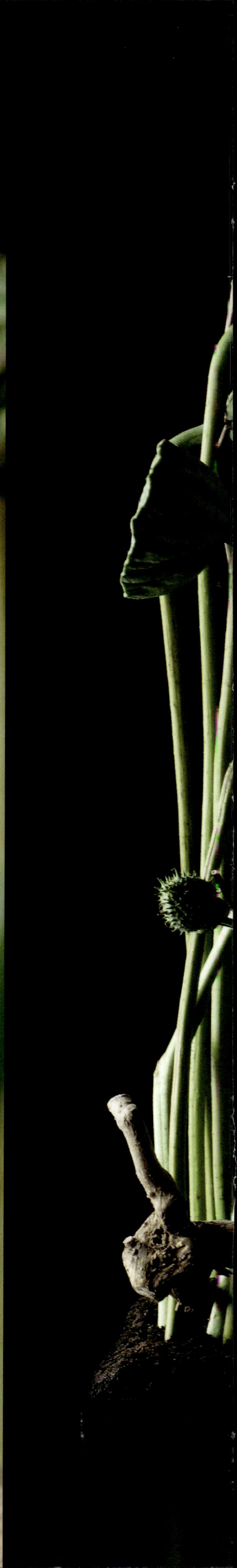

Datura stramonium f. stramonium / Nelumbo nucifera / Zantedeschia aethiopica

Fauna and Flora
Life and Life
come to an end
and softly cuddle each other
towards eternity.

Eucalyptus / Hydrangea macrophylla /
Juniperus communis subsp. communis / Leucadendron

Camellia japonica subsp. rusticana /
Cymbopogon citratus / Itea oldnamii /
Prunus mume

Paphiopedilum delenatii

Plants are beautiful and
stylish like jewels.
Embrace their personality,
to emphasize your individuality.

Hedera / Lactuca sativa / Orchidaceae (roots) / Tillandsia usneoides

60 | 61

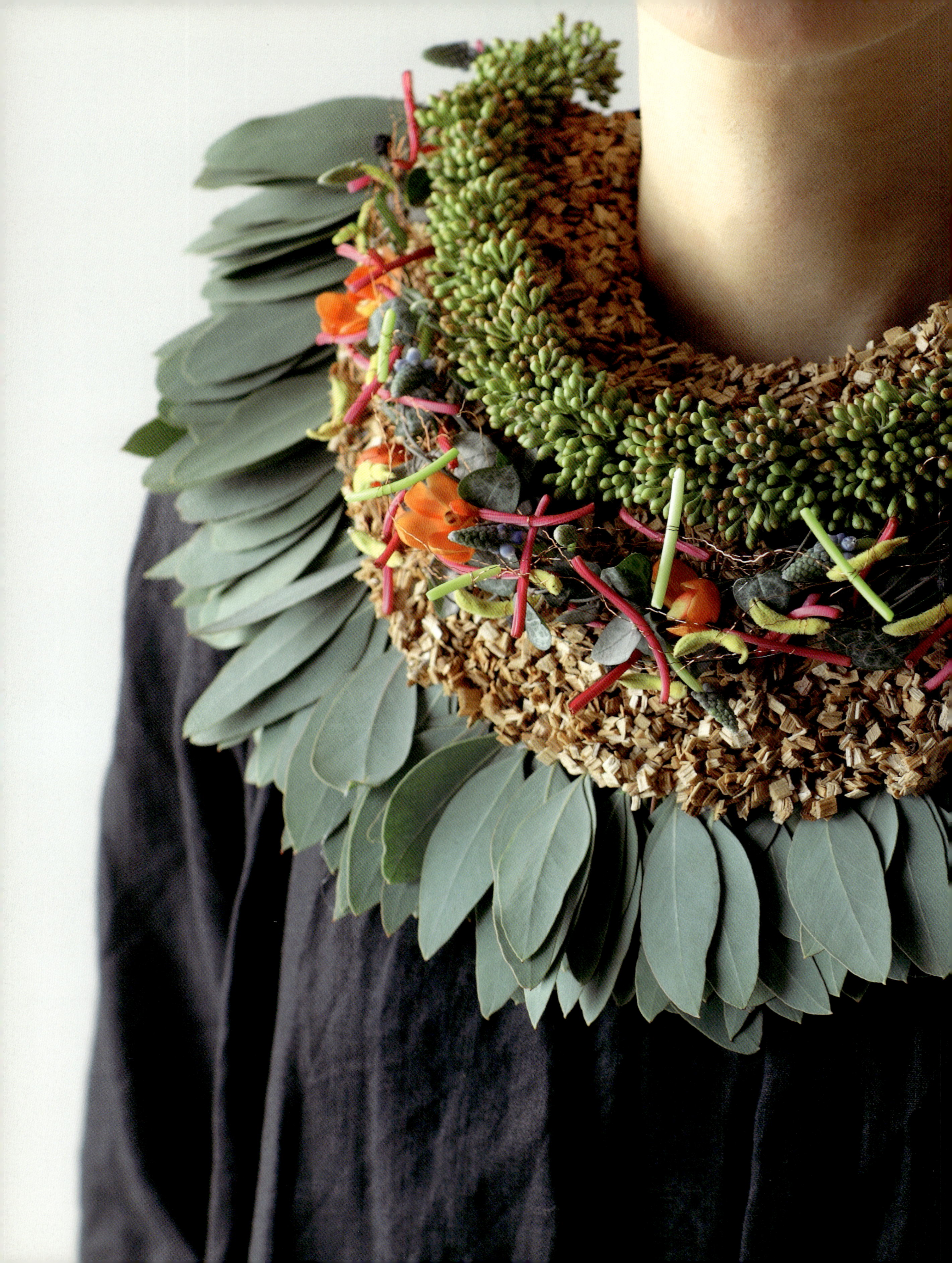

Anigozanthos / Ceropegia woodii / Eucalyptus / Hedera / Mokara / Muscari

Ipomoea / Oryza sativa subsp. javanica / Phalaenopsis / Phytolacca americana

64 | 65

Celosia cristata / Trichosanthes cucumeroides

66 | 67

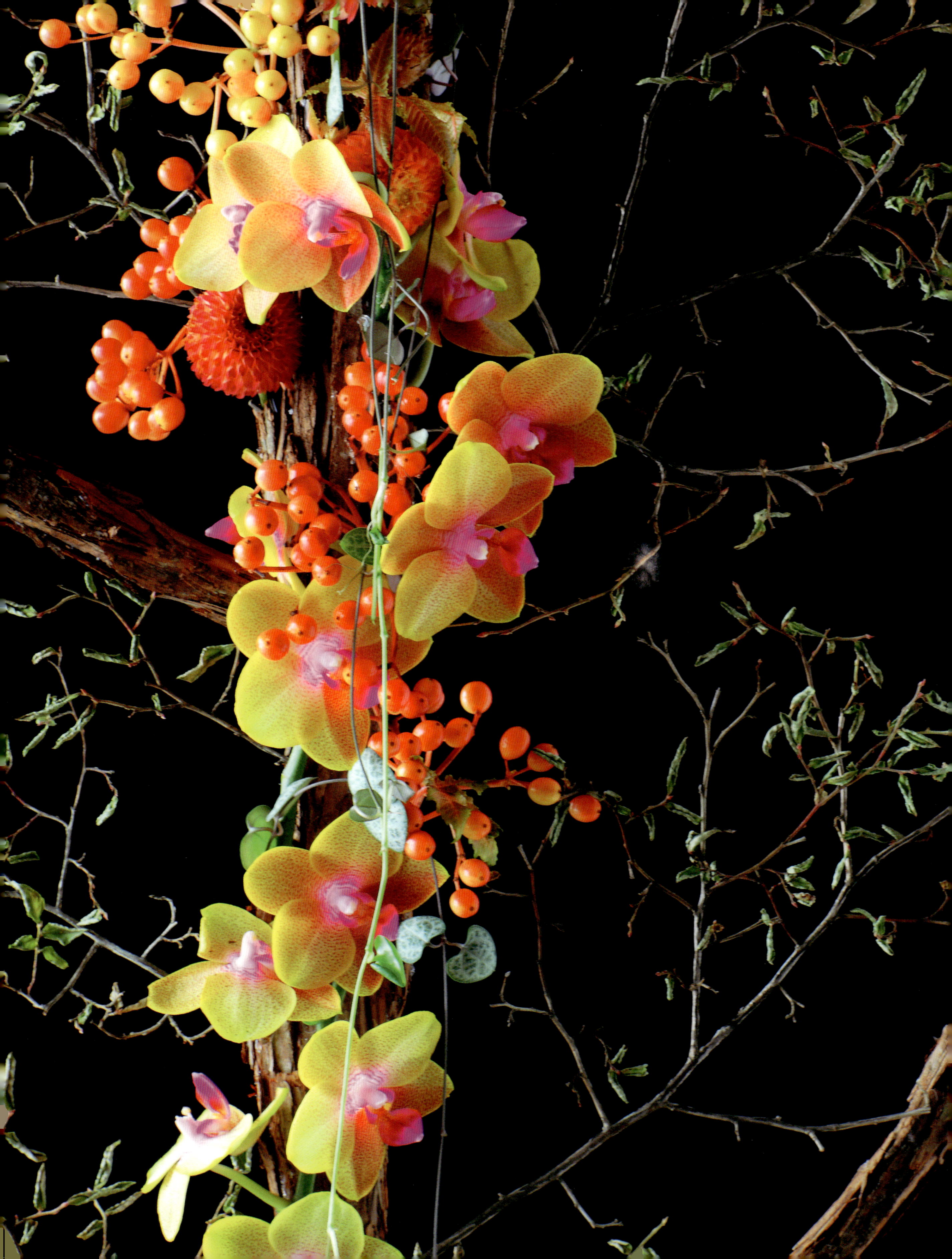

68 | 69

Begonia x rex-cultorum /
Ceropegia woodii /
Dahlia x cultorum / Phalaenopsis /
Viburnum compactum

Sensitive and beautiful orchids
afloat in the crystal sugar's sweet world.

Orchidaceae

70 | 71

Beautiful red and white,
traditional colors,
quintessentially Japanese.

Mokara / Nandina domestica / Paeonia lactiflora / Skimmia japonica

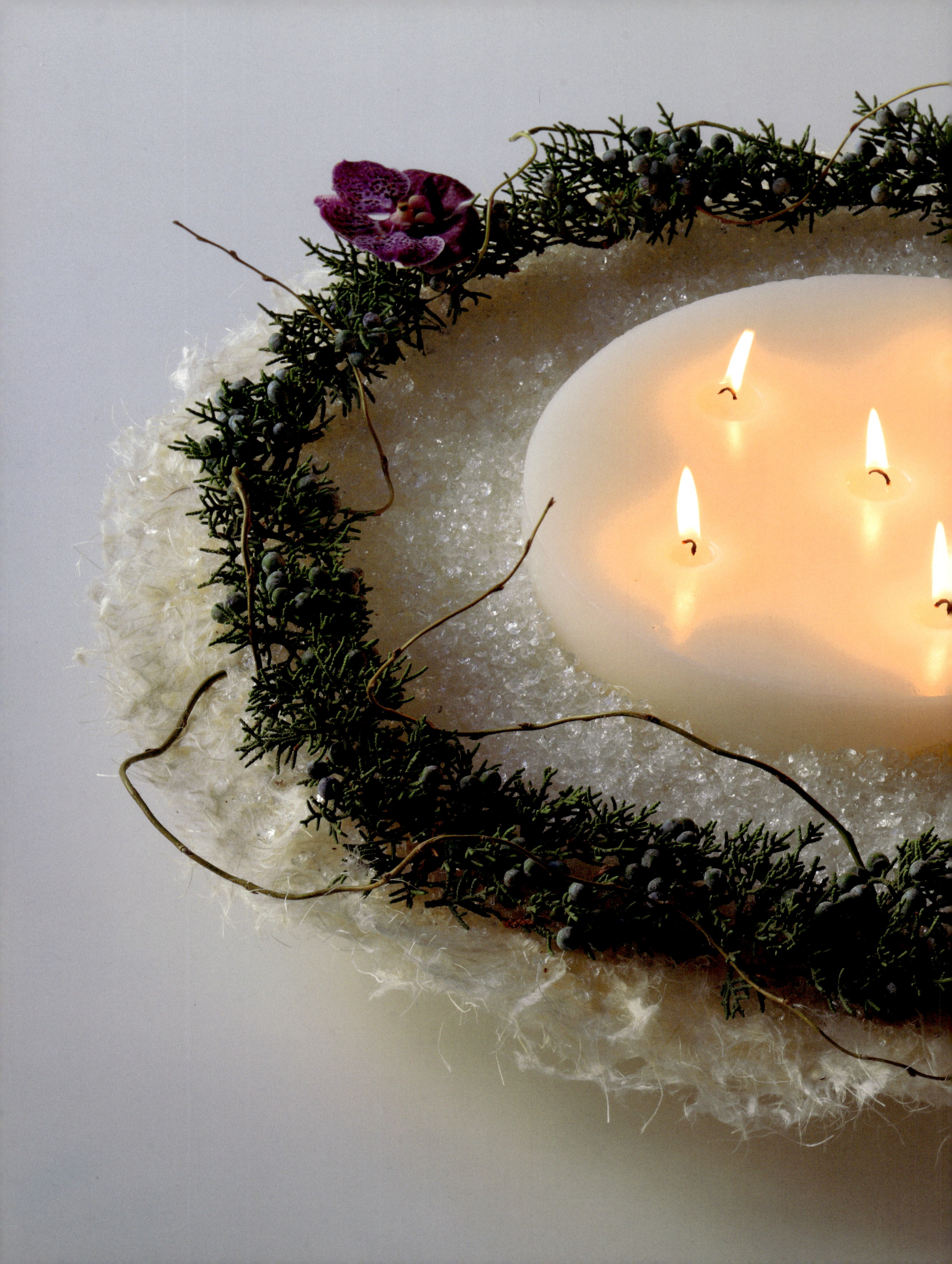

Juniperus communis subsp. communis / Salix matsudana / Vanda rothschildiana

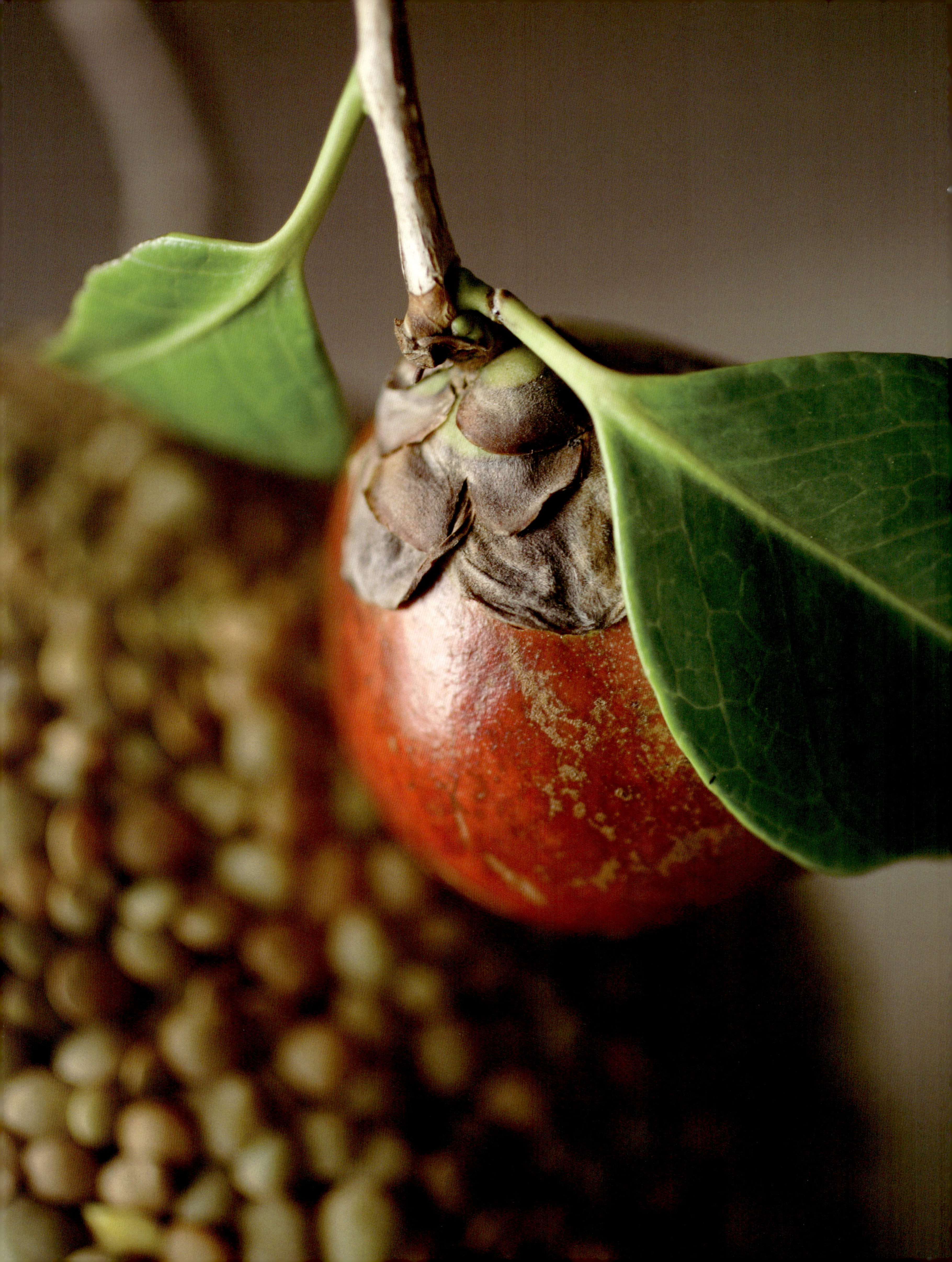

Camellia japonica / dried peas

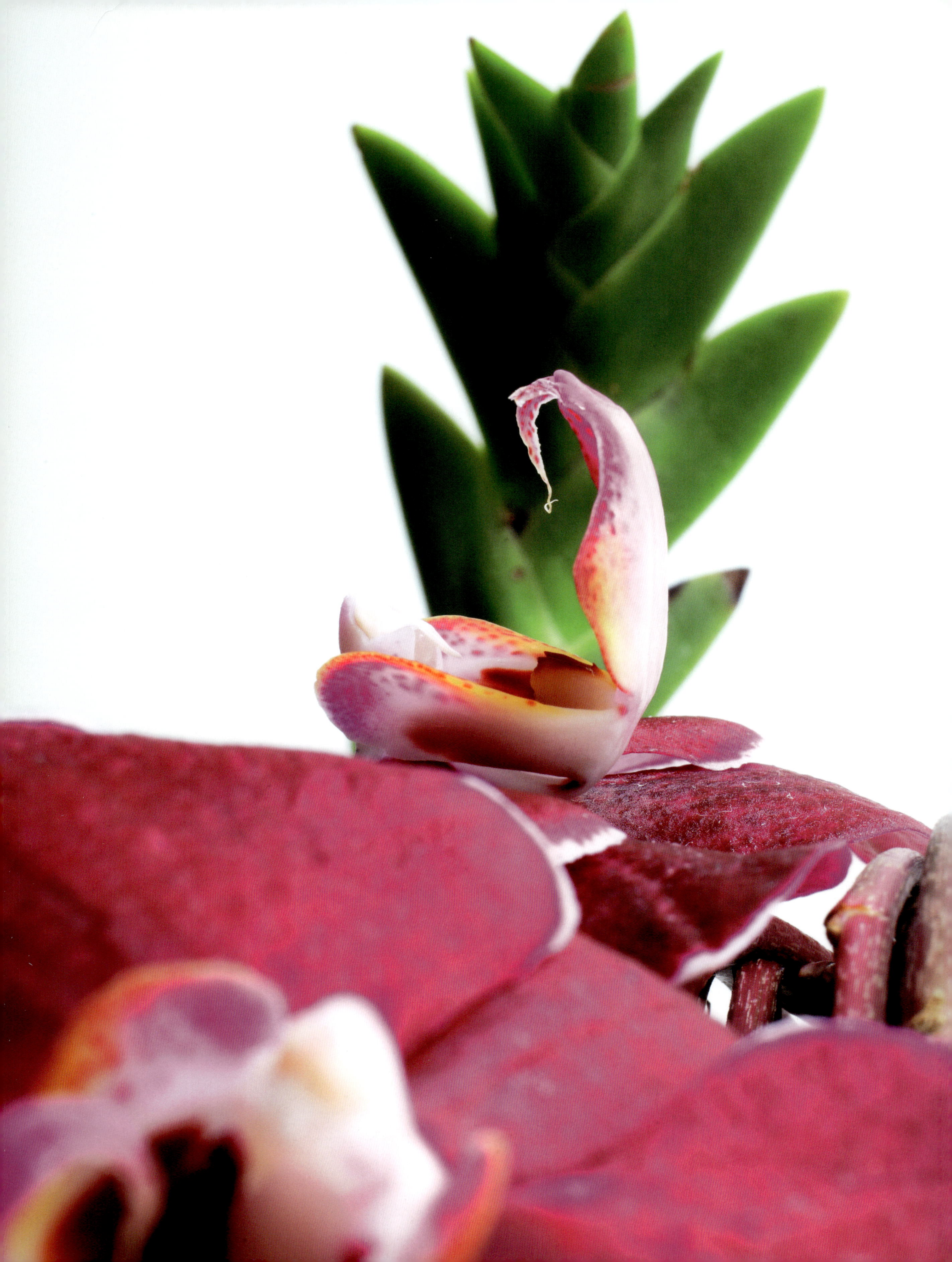

Hedera helix / Phalaenopsis / Pinus (needles)

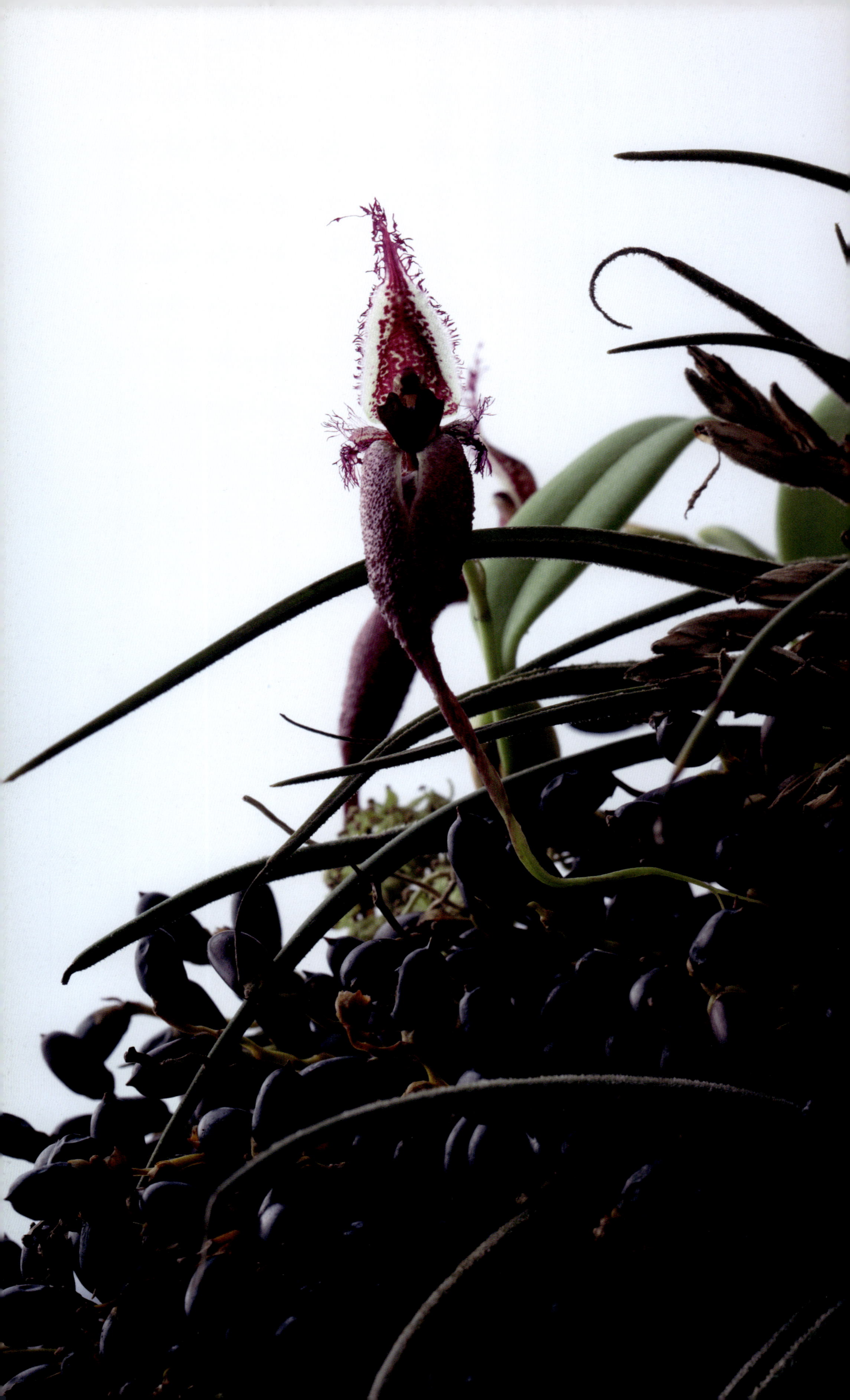

Eucalyptus / Orchidaceae / Phoenix roebelenii / Tillandsia

Aeonium arboreum / Eucalyptus / Rosa multiflora

82 | 83

Ephemeral beauty
highlighted
by the soft shimmer
of a flickering candle.

Lathyrus odoratus / Jasminum polyanthum

Lathyrus odoratus

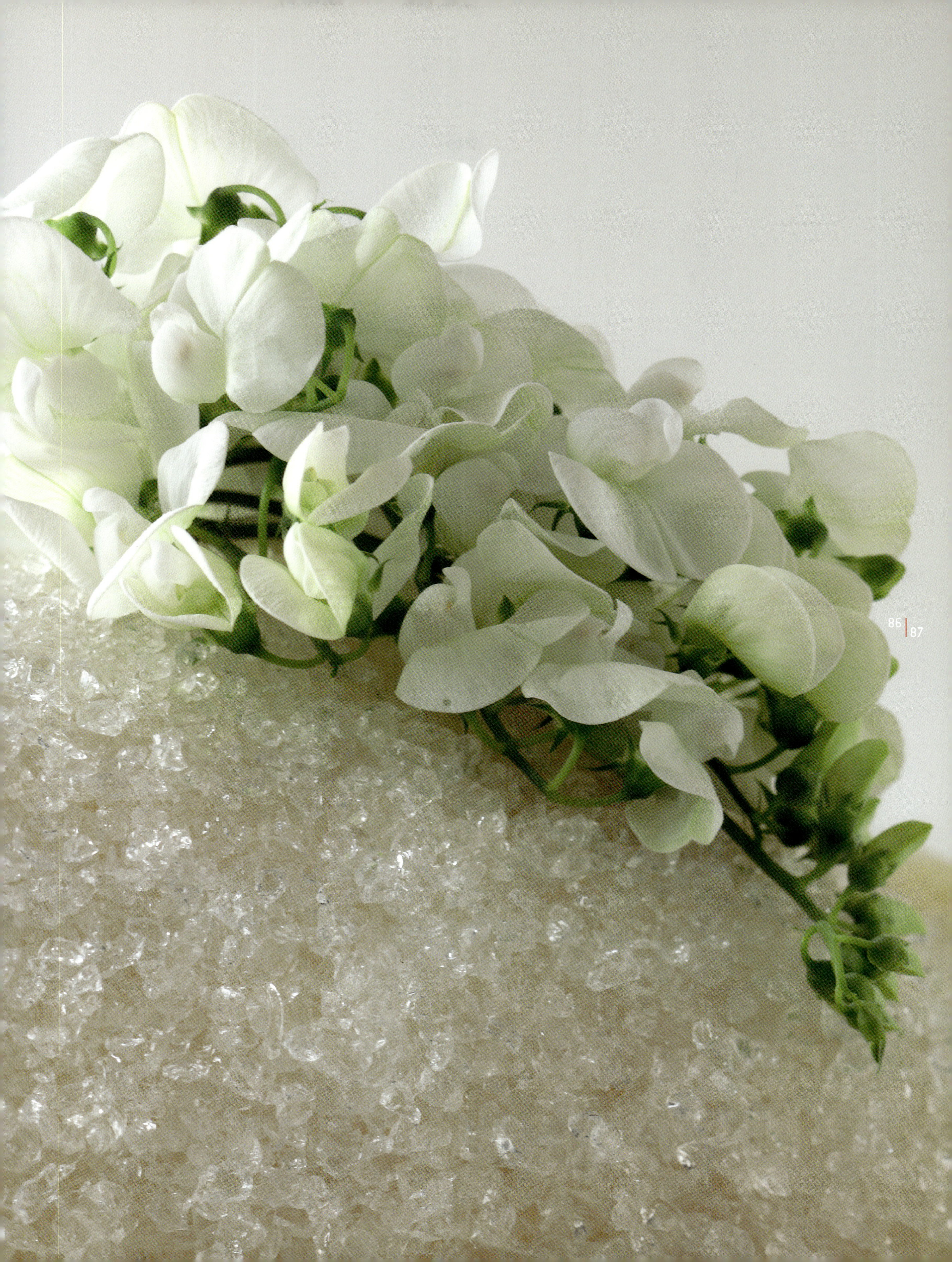

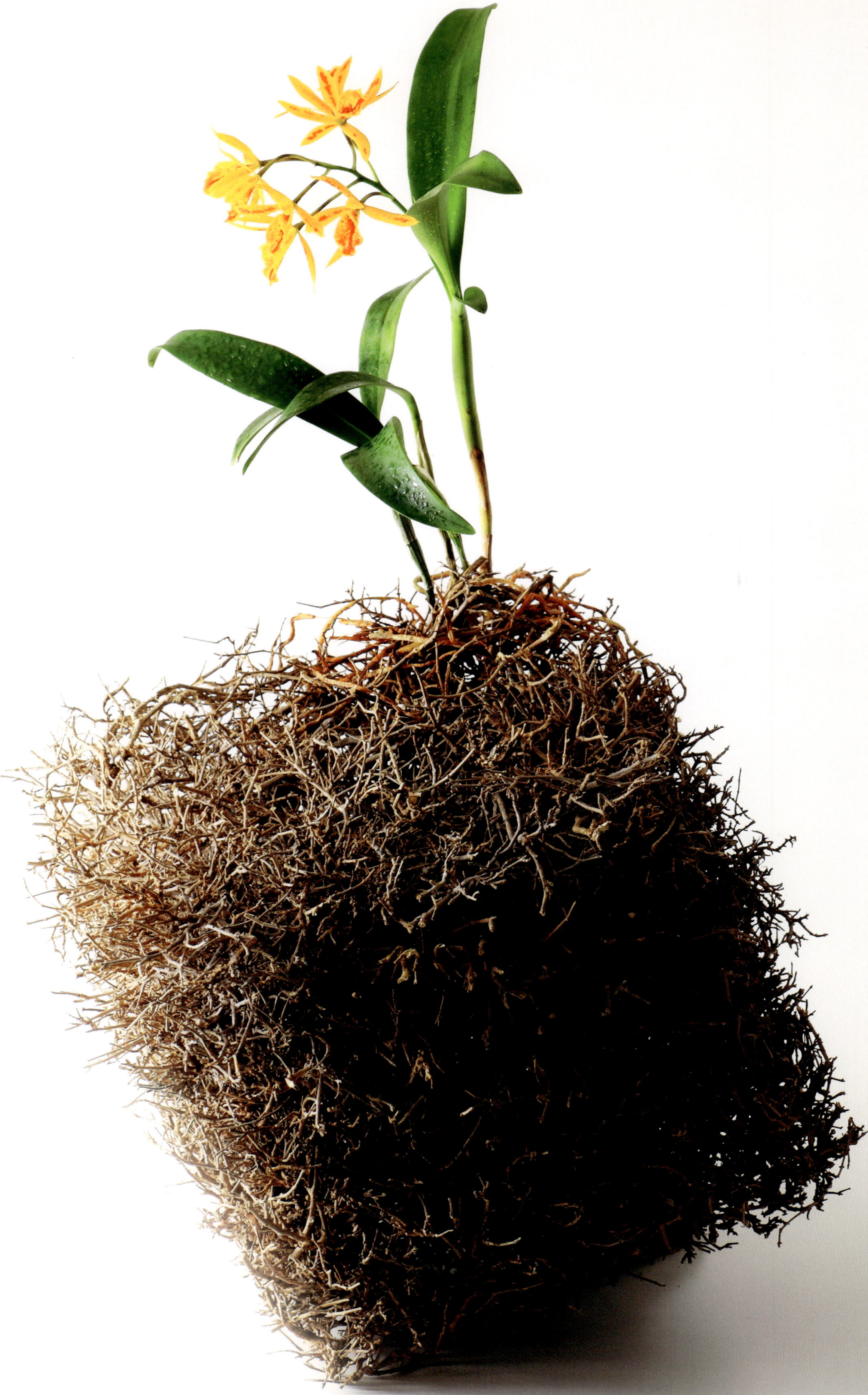

A cube of twigs and roots
supporting and nourishing
one blooming flower,
like Earth and Man.
History and future.

Epilaeliocattleya Don Herman 'Gold Rush'

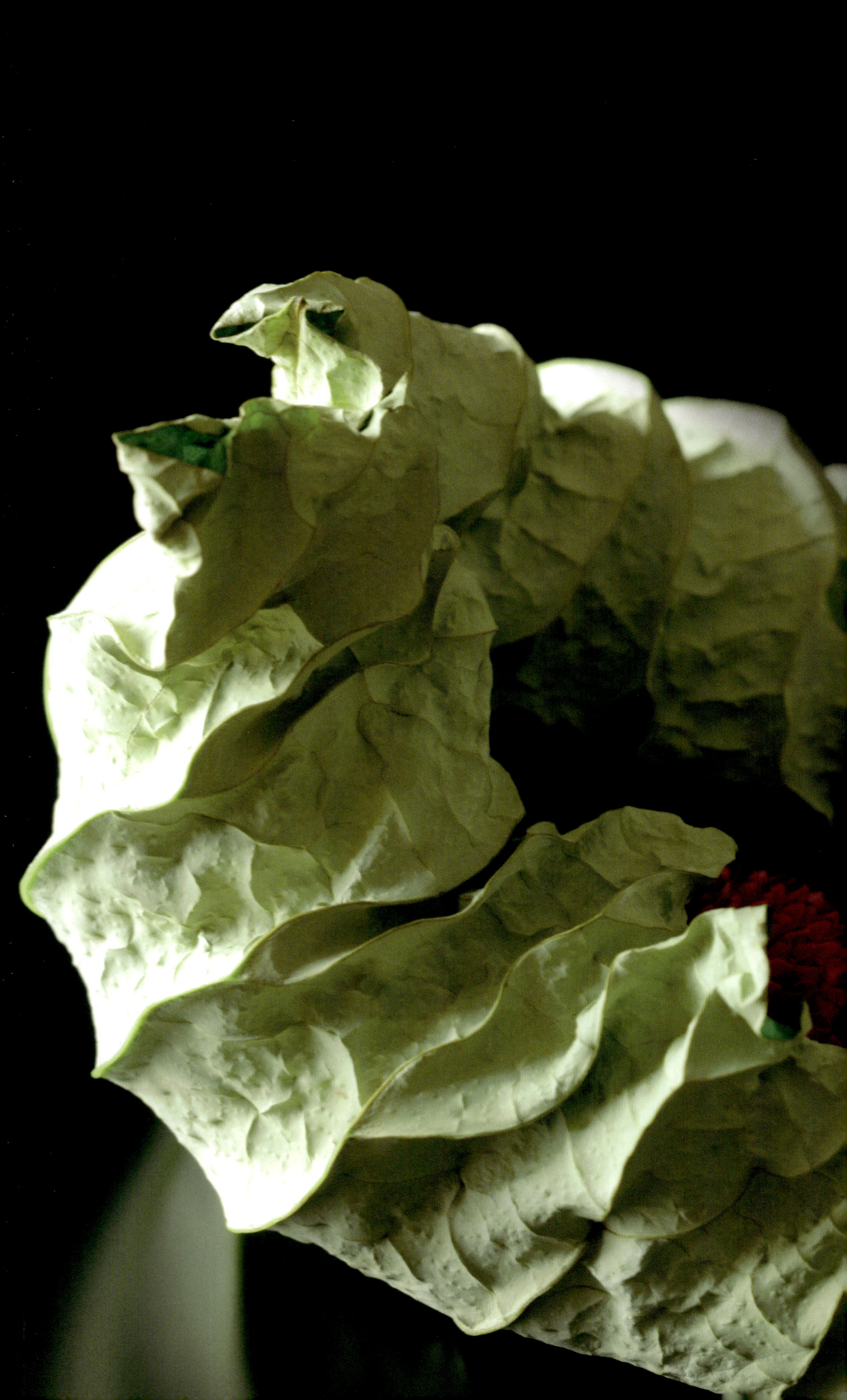

Capsicum annuum / Chrysanthemum morifolium / Nelumbo nucifera

Broken glass is useless
but proves a fertile ground for new life
and shines more beautiful than ever.

Cattleya

Yuko Takagi is founder and president of flower design school 'Quelle' (Motomachi, Kobe). She was awarded the National Trade Skill certification for flower decoration (first grade of Japan) and is first grade full-fledged member, head office teacher and test review member of the 'Nippon Flower Designers' Association'. She also works as a color coordinator and as a professional floral design instructor at Hana-ami school for floral design. Frequent travels bring her all over the world, where she teaches, gives demonstrations and workshops, and at the same time absorbs new trends in floral design. Her work is frequently featured in top class floristry magazines such as Fusion Flowers (UK), Florieren! (DE), Flowers& (US) and Flowers цветы (RUS).

Career highlights

1986 Started studying floral decoration
Studied English in Cambridge (UK)
Studied under royal warrant florist Kenneth Turner
Studied garden design in Cambridge

2000 Returned to Japan and studied under Kazumasa Kubo and Gabriele Wagner Kubo
Took several master classes with Gregor Lersch and served as an interpreter and assistant during his demonstrations in Japan
At Flower Festa Kobe in April 2000 she won 'The Chairman Award' of the Nippon Flower Designers' Association

2001 Winner of the Grand Prize at 'Kobe Flower Art Design'

2002 Japan Flower Design Award 2002, winner of the 1st prize in category 'Bouquet' and 'Silver Ribbon Award'
Demonstrated as a member of Hana-ami at the garden show in Stuttgart

2004 Japan Flower Design Award 2004, exhibited in 'Top Designer' category
Opening of flower school 'Quelle' in Motomachi, Kobe

2006 Invited as a Japanese designer to 'International Flower Exhibition' in Korea

2007 Exhibited as a Japanese designer during the IPM in Essen, Germany
Winner of the 'Golden Leaf' in the worldwide floral competition 'International Floral Art 06/07' (Stichting Kunstboek Publishers)
Seminar at a job training school in Copenhagen, Denmark
Interview appeared in the German magazine 'Florieren!'

2008 Demonstrated in the project of Nippon Flower Designers' Association (Hyogo branch)
3 works appeared in the 'International Floral Art 08/09' (Stichting Kunstboek Publishers)
Floral demonstration in Esbjerg, Denmark
Worked on the floral design for the grand opening of 'Dojima Hotel' (Osaka)
Worked on the design of main display in the lobby of ANA Crowne plaza Osaka
Design of the display in the lobby of ANA Crowne Plaza Osaka rebrand grand opening party

2009 Work appeared in the USA magazine 'Flowers&'
Won second prize in 'Hanging Design' category of the 'Philadelphia Flower Show'
Certified as 'International Teacher of Floristry' by the International Teachers of Floristry (Gregor Lersch)
Work appeared in 'Fusion Flowers' (UK)
Interview in 'Flowers цветы' (Russia)
Seminar given at the 'Garden club of America' (Houston, US)

2010 Demonstration during 'Japan Flower Design Award 2010'
3 designs published in the 'International Floral Art 2010/2011' (Stichting Kunstboek Publishers)
Work featured in 'Fusion Flowers'

94|95

Special thanks to

Tokuyo Takagi and Yumiko Takagi, my parents
Always in a good mood, gentle and continuously giving me generous affection.
I have carried on thanks to your support.
Keep walking besides me in good and hard times. I love you more than anything
in the world.

Takeshi Shirakawa, my husband
I am grateful for meeting you. You are an essential part of my life, always supportive
of me and my plans.
Many times when my heart was about to relent, you were gently by my side.
Thank you so much.

Haruyo Ihara, my grandmother
For teaching me everything about life, for being a beautiful, strong and gentle woman.
You were the one introducing me to the pleasure of creating things.

My photographer, Satoshi Shiozaki
You are the greatest, you understand my style to the smallest details.

Yu Nakano, my collaborator
For always supporting me and for striving for perfection. Thank you from my whole heart.

My translator, Tomoko Sugawara
My best friend for over 10 years, you are the sweetest.

Stiching Kunstboek, the publishers
For giving me this opportunity. Especially Katrien helped me a lot. I would like to show my
sincere appreciation.

My friends and colleagues all over the world.

CREATIONS & TEXTS
Yuko Takagi
2-2-14 Sakaemachi-dori Chuo-ku
650-0023 Kobe, Hyogo
Japan
www.quelle113.com
quelle@tea.ocn.ne.jp

PHOTOGRAPHY
Satoshi Shiozaki

FINAL EDITING
Katrien Van Moerbeke

LAY-OUT
www.groupvandamme.eu

PRINT
www.pureprint.be

PUBLISHED BY
Stichting Kunstboek bvba
Legeweg 165
B-8020 Oostkamp
T. +32 50 46 19 10
F. +32 50 46 19 18
info@stichtingkunstboek.com
www.stichtingkunstboek.com

ISBN 978-90-5856-360-6
D/2011/6407/12
NUR 421

All rights reserved. No part of this publication may be reproduced, stored in a database or retrieval system,
or transmitted in any form, or by any means, electronically, mechanically, by print, microfilm or otherwise
without prior permission in writing of the publisher.

© Stichting Kunstboek 2011